D0776765

ROMAN
MYTHOLOGY

Titles in the Mythology Series:

~ MYTHOLOGY ~

ROMAN MYTHOLOGY

Evelyn Wolfson

Enslow Publishers, Inc.

40 Industrial Road   PO Box 38
Box 398   Aldershot
Berkeley Heights, NJ 07922   Hants GU12 6BP
USA   UK

http://www.enslow.com

To Thea, Dacia, and John

Library of Congress Cataloging-in-Publication Data

Wolfson, Evelyn.
    Roman Mythology / Evelyn Wolfson.
        p. cm. – (Mythology)
    Includes bibliographical references and index.
    ISBN 0-7660-1558-0
    1. Mythology, Roman – Juvenile literature. [1. Mythology, Roman.] I. Title.
    II. Mythology (Berkeley Heights, N.J.)
    BL802 .W65 2001
    292.1'3—dc21   00-055147

Printed in the United States of America

10 9 8 7 6 5 4 3 2

To Our Readers: We have done our best to make sure all Internet addresses in
this book were active and appropriate when we went to press. However, the
author and the publisher have no control over and assume no liability for the
material available on those Internet sites or on other Web sites they may link to.
Any comments or suggestions can be sent by e-mail to comments@enslow.com
or to the address on the back cover.

Cover and Illustrations by William Sauts Bock

⊞ CONTENTS ⊞

Acknowledgments

My sincere and grateful thanks for expert advice, criticism, and comments to: Dr. Bennett Simon, classicist, psychoanalyst, author, and friend; and to Dacia Wolfson Callen, young classicist who took me on an archeological dig in Carthage and trekked many times over the years through Italy, Greece, and the islands of the Mediterranean and Aegean.

PREFACE

The Roman mythology we know today evolved over hundreds of years. Myths about the earliest Roman deities are different from most traditional myths that explain the actions of gods and goddesses or try to make sense of unexplainable events in nature. Roman myths give reasons for the rituals, ceremonies, and festivals held in honor of specific deities who represented important functions in daily life. The rituals, however, came first—then myths were created to go with the deities being honored.

Michael Grant, the author of *Roman Myths*, writes:

> In contrast to other peoples (Greeks, Germans, Celts) whose myths were stronger than their rites, the Roman rituals had survived wholly or largely without any mythological accompaniment; and as time went on an assortment of myths was brought in to "explain" them.[1]

Later, however, Roman myths began to resemble those of the Etruscans and Greeks, and early deities began to take on human form. These gods and goddesses also gained personalities and complex genealogies, or family trees.

In addition to myths about deities, the Romans also created two very popular myths about their own origins. One tells the story of the founding of Rome by Aeneas, a young Trojan whose mother was Venus, the goddess of love; and the other tells about the founding of Rome by Romulus, one of the twin sons of Mars, the god of agriculture and war. These myths appeared to read like history. *Roman Myths* author Michael Grant continues:

> Not only did they seek a chronological framework for all the events that had, in the historical sense, happened, but they

Atlantic Ocean

IRELAND

ENGLAND

FRANCE
ROMAN
CITY GATE →

GERMANY

S

SPAIN
ROMAN
AQUEDUCT
IN SPAIN
↓

ALPS

ROMAN
AQUEDUCT AT → • Nimes

ITALY

YUGOSLAVIA

Adria

AFRICA

Mediterranean

AFRICA

ROMAN TEMPLE
OF THE SIBYL →

ROME → ⊙

Tyrrhenian
Sea

← HEAD FROM ROMAN COIN

SICILY

Sea

ROMAN
EMPIRE

A
FR

RUINS OF
ROMAN HOUSE →

RUSSIA

HEAD OF ROMAN CHILD
FROM COIN

POLAND

IC PEOPLES

Vienna

RUSSIA

←ROMAN COIN

SCYTHIANS

Caspian Sea

PALACE OF DIOCLETIAN
IN YUGOSLAVIA

Black Sea

GREECE

Aegean Sea

ROMAN→
COLUMNS
on AEGEAN
COAST

ASIA
MINOR

N

W·E

S

SYRIA

CRETE

CYPRUS

PALESTINE

EGYPT

NILE R.

ARABIA

were just as eager to fit their mythical stories into an equally firm, connected sequence of pseudo-historical, pseudo-chronological narrative . . . [2]

Myths about the founding of Rome were written by historians and poets who wove science, fact, and fiction together to create believable stories that gave Romans a respectable ancestry. The Roman people placed a great deal of importance on their ancestral lines, and many kept detailed genealogies of their ancestors. Thus, Roman emperors were eager to have an immortal in their background, and many of them were eventually worshipped in the same manner as gods. One emperor joked on his deathbed, "Oh dear, I think I'm becoming a god."[3]

The Roman poet Virgil had little difficulty relating the heroic battles of Aeneas' struggle to found Lavinium with Rome's victorious wars during the early years of the Republic, the Punic Wars, and the period of the Roman Empire. He wrote convincingly about these wars and other events using only snippets of history, and when wars did not fit properly into his story, he transformed current events into ancient ones.

The Land

The Italian peninsula extends out into the Mediterranean Sea and is often referred to as "the boot," due to its boot-like shape. The country is surrounded on three sides by water: the Tyrrhenian Sea on the west, the Ionian Sea on the south, and the Adriatic Sea on the east. The Apennine mountain range dominates the central portion of the peninsula. On the western side of the Apennines, in the northernmost part of Italy and at the foot of the Alps, the valley formed by the Po River creates a rich, fertile plain. On the eastern side of the mountains, rolling hills give way to a broad coastal plain that borders the Adriatic Sea. The Tiber, the largest river in Italy, bisects the western coastal plain. The Tiber is broad as it flows out of the mountains, but it narrows as it courses across the plain. The area of the plain south of the Tiber River, including present-day Rome, was once known as Latium.

Archaeological evidence has revealed that the first people settled in Latium sometime during the eleventh century B.C. They were seminomadic tribesmen who came from central Europe and who spoke an Indo-European language. On the Latium plain they found good pasturage for their flocks of sheep and fertile soil for farming on the Alban Hills, fifteen miles southeast of present-day Rome. Monte Cavo, the highest peak in the area, offered a good view of the surrounding plain.

By 850 B.C., some of the tribesmen had migrated to the site of present-day Rome. This area included seven flat-topped hills that curved outward toward the Tiber River. The most northerly hills were the Quirinal, Viminal, Esquiline, and Caelian. Between these hills and the Tiber River stood the steep Palatine Hill and the even steeper Capitoline Hill. To the south of these stood the Aventine Hill. A broad, swampy area between the Palatine and Capitoline hills was agriculturally unproductive until the area was drained centuries later.

The first settlement was in the area of what eventually became the city of Rome. The site was the steep two-crested Palatine Hill, which offered good protection from attack and was the closest hill to a natural crossing of the Tiber River. These early farmers and shepherds planted crops of wheat, millet, and barley in the rich volcanic soils around the hills and grazed their sheep on nearby hilly pastures. Men built small round or elliptical huts and covered them with reeds, twigs, and clay. Then, they

Tiber River

GOAT'S MARSH

early hut of reeds
and twigs plaster
with cla

PANTHEON

CAPITOLINE HILL

QUIRINAL HILL

VIMINAL HILL

TIBERINE ISLAND

Sublician Bridge

early hut villages

PALATINE HILL

ESQUILINE HILL

Velian Isthmus

FORUM
ARCH OF TITUS

COLOSSEUM

ARCH OF CONSTANTINE

EMPLE

AVENTINE HILL   CAELIAN HILL

Aene

City of
ROME

surrounded their hilltop settlements with earthen ramparts, or protective barriers, that were later replaced by stone. These settlers of the seven hills eventually became known as the Latins.

Another group of tribesmen, the Sabines, had by 1000 B.C. already settled near the foothills of the Apennines. The Sabines spoke a different version of the Indo-European language than did the Latins. Eventually, the Sabines met their Latin neighbors where they pastured their sheep together. In time, the Sabines came to live on the Esquiline and Quirinal hills. Gradually, the Sabines became united with the Latins as their settlements on the seven hills grew closer together.

Early settlers utilized the Tiber River for transportation and trade, and a growing class of merchants and artisans began to emerge. Other parts of Italy were being colonized at the same time. One of the largest settlements, established by the Greeks around 750 B.C., was at Cumae near the Bay of Naples.

The Etruscans

A century or two before the Latins settled on the south side of the Tiber River, another group settled on the north side in a region called Etruria. The people of Etruria, called Etruscans, were more advanced than their Latin neighbors, and they greatly influenced Latin culture. The Etruscans established city-states, or communities, that administered their own affairs. Believed to have emigrated from Lydia in Asia Minor, they did not speak an Indo-European language and no written records or literature belonging to the Etruscans has ever been found. The ancient Romans called the people of the region "Tusci," from which is derived the modern name of the Italian region known as Tuscany.[4]

During the seventh century, as Latin communities on the south side of the Tiber were beginning to coalesce, Etruscan city-states on the north side were becoming strong and powerful. Eventually, the Etruscans conquered Campania and Latium. For the next 150 years, Rome was under Etruscan control.

Early Roman Religion

The early Romans were farmers and shepherds who spent most of their time outdoors. They did not understand why droughts and floods periodically plagued them; why lightning struck; or why, in general, the conditions of their world were so unpredictable. Yet these mysterious forces greatly affected their lives. As a result, they began to worship and make offerings to a variety of spirit forces, or deities, that they believed dwelled all around them—in the fields and forests and in their homes. These mysterious powers were so vague that the people could not envision them in any real shape or gender, so they did not create human forms to represent them. Unlike the Greek gods and goddesses, who had strong personalities and humanlike figures, these early Roman deities were only ideas and did not take any physical form. To protect themselves from evil influences and to secure the goodwill of these seemingly powerful deities, the early Romans worshipped at simple altars, upon which they left offerings of food, wine, and incense.

Early Roman Deities

Because early deities were idolized for the purposes they served and farming occupied much of the people's time, agricultural deities were very important. Ceres, the most honored of the farming deities, was believed to watch over the planting of the grain. (The word "cereal" is derived from *Ceres*.) In January, Ceres would be honored during the festival of the "Sowing of the Seed." During the farming season, farmers would give each of their actions a name to ensure that the activity would be aided by the energy of the deity whose name it had been assigned. According to the Romans, Robigus was the personification of wheat rust and spared the grains; Flora caused the plants to blossom; Consus protected the stored grains and Quirinus was celebrated in the fall when grains were roasted.[5]

Mars and Saturn were also important deities associated with the fertility of the land. Mars, god of agriculture, later became associated with Ares, the Greek god of war; and Saturn, god of agriculture and time, became associated with the Greek god Cronus, father of Zeus (whose name means "sown"). Saturnalia, a festival that honored Saturn and his consort Ops, the Italian goddess of plenty, was celebrated each year from December 17 to December 23. During that week, trade was closed down, slaves were given temporary freedom, families exchanged gifts, and everyone enjoyed a period of feasting.

Other early deities represented the practical needs of everyday life. Janus, a Roman god with no Greek equivalent, was worshipped at doorways. People would pray to him before leaving to ensure a safe journey, and before entering to prevent evil spirits from coming through the door after it had been opened. During the third and fourth centuries B.C., after Rome had become a prosperous city, Janus became the guardian of the gates of the city. In times of peace, the gates were kept closed to keep peace from escaping; and during wartime, the gates would remain open to allow Roman soldiers to march through when they returned from battle. Janus was depicted as a man with two faces, one facing forward and the other facing backward, to be able to preside over both exits and entrances. He became the god of beginnings and the custodian of the universe. His name was always invoked first in prayer, and he held sacred the first hour of the day, the first day of the month, and the first month of the year. Legends attribute Janus' status as the god of beginnings to Numa Pompilius, the second king of Rome. In the eighth century B.C., King Numa added two months to the beginning of the old ten-month calendar and named the first new month *Januarius*, after the god Janus. Today, we call the first month of the year January.[6]

The Lares were protective deities of the land. They dwelled in the fields, at sacred crossroads, and where several farms came together. The Lares were always associated with a particular place. At the beginning of January, the Lares were honored during the festival of Compitalia. At this time, farmers would put up towers where their lands intersected. These towers had doors that faced each of the adjacent farms. Farmers often built altars there, and this creative tower-altar arrangement allowed farmers to stand on their own property while making sacrifices and offerings to the Lares.[7]

While the Lares protected all members of a household whether they were related or not, the Penates guarded the master of the house and his family exclusively. In exchange for well-stocked cupboards and continued good health, the people prayed and made offerings at indoor altars to the Penates.[8]

Pales, guardian spirit of the flock, protected and watched over the sheep after they were moved from winter pastures in the valleys to summer pastures in the hills. He also brought the animals good health, an abundance of grass and water, and insured good wool and milk.[9] Pales was honored in April during the festival of Parilia, before the sheep were moved from their winter to their summer pastures.

In a primitive world where fires were lit by rubbing two sticks together, Vesta, guardian of the hearth, was an important deity. The fires of Vesta were never allowed to go out in the crude huts of the early Romans. Each day, the youngest daughter of a family would make offerings of salted cakes to Vesta to ensure a continuous fire. Vesta, like Janus, eventually became an important goddess of the city. A round, hutlike structure was built in Rome to house the fire of Vesta permanently, and it came to represent the hearth of Rome. Although no human form was ever made to represent her, Vesta became a goddess image attended by women called Vestal Virgins. Vestal Virgins were responsible for keeping the fire of Vesta burning at all times. If the fire were to go out, it would be considered a warning that some great evil would befall Rome and its people. These young women, chosen from prestigious Roman families, enjoyed all the privileges afforded to diplomats and wealthy Romans. For the privilege of tending the fire of Vesta, the young women vowed to remain chaste for thirty years, after which they could leave the cloister and get married. The penalty for breaking their vows, however, was to be buried alive.

In addition to the deities of the living world, the Romans never neglected the spirits of their dead relatives. In May, during the festival of Lemuria, families conducted private ceremonies at home to gain the good will of lemures, the wandering spirits of their dead relatives. At that time, the head of the family tossed beans over his shoulder as offering to the spirits.[10]

Kings of Rome

For 150 years, a period of time that stretched across the entire sixth century B.C., the city of Rome was under Etruscan control. The conquest of Alba Longa fifteen miles

southeast of Rome was believed to have occurred during the time of the Etruscan kings. There were seven legendary rulers, or kings, of Rome: The first king, Romulus, instituted the Senate; the second king, Numa Pompilius, established priesthoods; the third king, Tullus Hostilius, expanded Rome's influence and glory through war; and the fourth king, Ancus Marcius, established procedures for declaring war. The remaining kings included the fifth, Tarquinius Priscus; the sixth, Servius Tullius; and the seventh, Tarquinius Superbus.[11]

The first Etruscan king, Tarquinius Priscus, was of Greek descent, and he focused on reforming the army. Priscus also built a temple on the Capitol to honor Jupiter, Juno, and Minerva. These three deities, known as the Capitoline Triad, held a supreme place in Roman religion. Chapter 1 of this text elaborates on the Capitoline Triad because these deities figure prominently in the historical myths about the founding of Rome by Aeneas and Romulus.

The sixth king, Servius Tullius (578–534 B.C.), organized Roman society by rank and divided the population into classes. Men who owned property had political power and could join the military. He also established the earliest and most important shrine of the Latin deity Diana on the Aventine Hill.[12] Diana was concerned with the affairs of women and later became associated with the Greek goddess Artemis, who was the goddess of the moon and hunting.

The seventh and last king, Tarquinius Superbus, or Tarquin the Proud, was not elected legally and was not well liked because he made the Romans do manual labor for public works. He was dethroned in 509 B.C. According to legend, he tried to purchase from the Sibyl at Cumae the Sibylline Books, a set of nine books that contained all of

Apollo's prophecies of the world. (A *sibyl* is a soothsayer or someone who foretells future events by some sort of supernatural means; Cumae is a port along the southern coast of Italy.) Apollo had given the books to the Sibyl and had offered to grant her anything she desired if she would marry him. The Sibyl agreed on the one condition that he grant her as many years of life as grains of sand she could hold in one hand. After Apollo granted the Sibyl her wish, she quickly reneged on her promise. Apollo then reminded the Sibyl that because she had forgotten to ask to remain ageless, he was going to withhold that gift. The Sibyl of Cumae lived on as an old woman for more than seven hundred years, until only her small, weak voice survived to hand down Apollo's world prophecies.[13]

When Tarquin the Proud asked to purchase the books from the Sibyl, she agreed to sell them to him—but he refused to pay her price. So the Sibyl burned three of the nine books. A year later, the Sibyl offered the king the remaining six books at the same price. Still, he refused to pay her price, so she burned three more of the books. Exasperated, Tarquin the Proud finally agreed to pay the original price for the remaining three books.

The early Romans did not adapt easily to existing Etruscan religious practices. The Etruscans followed the reading of omens by their priests. In these readings, the priests, or augurs, interpreted for the people the meaning of messages from the gods, believed to be hidden in the flight patterns of birds or in the color and consistency of animals' entrails.[14]

Over the centuries, many Greeks and Carthaginians came to live in Etruria, and the Etruscans readily embraced many aspects of their cultures. The Etruscans, in turn, introduced a civilized and prosperous way of life to the Romans. Many Greek gods and goddesses were absorbed into the growing body of Roman deities. Jupiter became the Roman equivalent of Zeus, the Greek king of the gods (Jupiter even adopted Zeus' symbols of power—lightning bolts and peals of thunder); Juno became the Roman equivalent of Hera, Zeus' wife; and Venus became the Roman equivalent of Aphrodite, the Greek goddess of beauty.

In the beginning, when Roman deities became identified with Greek gods and goddesses, they did not interact with humans in Roman myths because the Romans were not comfortable with the Greek idea of divine intervention in their stories. Eventually, however, this attitude changed and humans and divinities began to interact in Roman myths just as they did in Greek myths.

Mars, Venus, and Apollo are included in Chapter 2 because these deities also play an important part in the myths about the founding of Rome.

The Republic

After Tarquinius Superbus was overthrown in 510 B.C., Rome became a republic, or a self-governing state. The Etruscans tried to regain power over the Romans, but they failed each time they tried. (Rome eventually conquered Etruria in 218 B.C.)

As a republic, the Roman people voted men into office to carry out the affairs of government. To make sure that no one man held all the power, the Romans appointed consuls (two or more men who shared the same job). Women were never allowed to participate in politics or government. Two classes of people eventually evolved in Rome: the patricians, or nobles, who represented the privileged ruling class, and the plebeians, or commoners, who made up the working class.

During the period of the Republic, the Romans fought

many wars against both invading tribes and their Latin neighbors. A devastating war was fought against the Gauls, a Celtic people, in 387 B.C. Legendary sources say that the Gauls were bribed with gold to leave Rome after they sacked and burned the city. Romans lost most, or all, of their official records in this fire.

By 341 B.C., however, the Romans ruled most of Italy and Latin-speaking people began to learn Greek from Greek colonists in southern Italy, Sicily, and elsewhere in the Mediterranean area. The Romans granted the gods of most of the territories they conquered the same honors they gave their own deities. For some time, however, the Romans banned the worship of eastern deities and would not allow the cults who worshipped them to reside in Rome. Then, in 204 B.C., the Great Mother, or Magna Mater, from present-day Turkey (Asia Minor) was introduced to the Romans. Although the ceremonial music and dance honoring the Great Mother were almost too exotic for the Romans, she became a native deity because her homeland of Asia Minor was believed to be the original homeland of the Roman people.[15]

At about the same time, the Egyptian goddess Isis, the eternal wife and mother, was introduced to Rome. Isis was worshipped, and she enjoyed greater popularity than the Great Mother.

As Roman power was growing in Italy and the eastern Mediterranean, the Carthaginians, a Phoenician people originally from Tyre (a city on the present-day coast of Lebanon) were gaining control in the western Mediterranean. They established a powerful city and port at Carthage in northern Africa (present-day Tunisia). The growth of power in Sicily and aggressive military operations in the Mediterranean so angered the Romans that they fought the Phoenicians in the Punic Wars from

264 B.C. to 146 B.C. *Punic* is the Latin word for "Phoenician." The Romans emerged as the victors of the Punic Wars after the destruction of Carthage in 146 B.C. Most notable of the participants was Hannibal, a courageous and skillful Carthaginian warrior.

During the Punic Wars, Rome experienced many internal power struggles, particularly between the patricians, or nobles, and plebeians, or peasants. Finally, civil war broke out during the first century B.C., and Julius Caesar ultimately became dictator.

The Empire

Julius Caesar (100–44 B.C.) and his adopted son Octavian (63 B.C.–A.D. 14) became the most widely known and esteemed members of the Julian family, or clan. Caesar struggled to hold on to his power and to institute social reforms in Rome, but he was eventually assassinated in 44 B.C. In 27 B.C., Octavian became the first emperor of Rome. Octavian changed his name to *Augustus*, meaning "majestic" in Latin, and his reign lasted until his death. During his reign, and for four hundred years thereafter, democracy as it had been known under the Republic ceased to exist. Still, Augustus worked with members of the former Republican government, and eventually the empire grew stable and prosperous. He was able to achieve peace at home while promoting the growth of an empire that included most of modern Europe. Said one historian, "The Romans believed that their empire was acquired with the help of the gods, who rewarded Roman piety [devotion to family and state] with military victories."

Augustus was a great supporter of the arts and culture, and of historians and poets. He worked hard to restore the ancient religious festivals of the Romans. Augustus claimed to be descended from Aeneas, a legendary founder of Rome, whose mother was the goddess Venus. The Romans had become so convinced of his divinity that when a comet appeared after Caesar's death, people believed it was his spirit rising to heaven.[17]

Language

During the first four centuries A.D., when the Roman Empire dominated most of Europe, Latin was the official language of each new territory. Originally spoken in and around Rome, Latin soon extended with Roman rule over much of ancient Europe. Some inhabitants of conquered territories continued to speak their own languages. Others began to combine their own languages with the less sophisticated language of the Roman soldiers and peasants who came to live among them. A fusion of different dialects eventually grew into the languages of modern Europe that we know today, such as French, Portuguese, Spanish, Italian, and Romanian.[18]

Although archaic Latin inscriptions began to appear on stone as early as 600 B.C., few uses of a written language appeared before the third century B.C. Oral Latin, however, had been widely used from the earliest times.

Literary Sources of Roman Myths

Although civil wars had plagued the Republic in the first century B.C., a great deal of literary activity took place toward the end of the century. A period called the Golden Age of Roman Literature began to develop in 70 B.C., and from 43 B.C. until A.D. 14, literature truly flourished under Emperor Augustus.

Romans had long been absorbing mythological stories about gods and goddesses from other parts of the world, but they wanted a mythology of their own. The Roman poet Ovid (43 B.C.–A.D. 17) began to research and record the mythology of early Roman deities. Ovid, like other great poets of his time, used as much historical information as he could find but also relied on his creative imagination. His greatest work, *Metamorphoses*, is a fifteen-volume epic poem that includes tales about early Roman gods and goddesses, although their stories are taken mostly from the Greek. At the same time that Ovid was composing *Metamorphoses*, he was also composing another poem, *Fasti*, a lyrical version of the Roman calendar that became the primary source of information about early Roman deities. *Fasti* presents many of the sacred rites and festivals of the Roman religious year beginning with the month of January. Unfortunately, only the first six months of this calendar were completed.

In the first century B.C., the historian Livy (59 B.C.–A.D. 17) laboriously composed the *History of Rome* on long rolls of papyrus, a type of paper made from plant fibers. Of the 142 volumes he wrote, only one quarter of them have survived in their entirety; pieces of all but two of the others also survive. Several of the surviving volumes included semilegendary accounts of the founding and history of Rome beginning in 753 B.C. Livy had garnered as much information as possible from early histories of Rome written by Greek and Latin authors, from Roman and Etruscan family genealogies, and from the records of early priests. Neither the early Romans nor the Etruscans kept organized written records, so much of the time Livy had to rely on his imagination. Livy intended to show that Rome's modest beginnings exhibited greatness right from the start. His narrative provided convincing background for the glories of the Augustan age.[19]

The Roman poet Virgil (70–19 B.C.) was composing poetry at the same time that Livy was writing history, although they worked independently. Virgil began composing *The Aeneid* after Livy had finished the first of his 142 volumes of history. *The Aeneid* tells about the founding of Lavinium by Aeneas, a young Trojan whose mother is Venus, goddess of love, and whose father is a mortal Trojan named Anchises. Virgil weaves a mythological tale around the destruction of Troy, an ancient city in northwest Asia Minor (present-day Turkey) in 1250 B.C., and Aeneas' journey to find a new homeland for the Trojan people. Virgil's poem is a literary masterpiece filled with adventure, romance, and tragedy.

Virgil, the son of a middle-class farmer, studied in Rome and Naples as well as in Greece. He became fluent in both Latin and Greek and was well-versed in the histories of Greece and Rome. Virgil studied the works of the Greek poet Homer, who had written *The Iliad* and *The Odyssey* during the eighth century B.C., about 700 years earlier. Homer's epic poems dealt with the legendary events that were believed to have occurred in the early twelfth century in the city of Troy.

For many years, historians believed that Troy was a fictitious city. Then, in the late nineteenth century, German archaeologist Hermann Schliemann uncovered the remains of a city in the same location described by Homer. The city is believed to have been ancient Troy, which was situated along a forty-mile-long stretch of waterway, the Dardanelles, connecting the Marmara and Aegean seas. The city had commercial control over the Dardanelles and was probably a wealthy and bustling center of trade at the time it was destroyed. No written history of a real war has ever been found.

However, the earliest legendary accounts of a war traced the origin of the Trojan War to the abduction of Helen, the wife of King Menelaus of Sparta (a territory in

Greece) by a Trojan prince named Paris. When the Trojans refused to return Helen, the Greek world went to war. The fighting lasted for ten years, until the Greeks finally sacked and burned Troy.

There are two popular stories about Roman origins: Aeneas' founding of Rome and Romulus' founding of Rome. The chronology of Virgil's poem, however, presented a problem to scholars during the third century when they began to research and write about early Roman history. Virgil's myth indicates a time gap of almost five hundred years between the time Aeneas arrived in Lavinium and the date given for the founding of Rome. Assuming that the date of the end of the Trojan War was 1250 B.C., it would have been impossible for Aeneas to have been the founder of Rome in 753 B.C. To fill in the time gap, historians and poets created a mythology of kings who may or may not have been real. As a result, the history and mythology associated with the origins of the Roman people and the founding of Rome became flexible, and chronology was not considered important. The dates attributed to the various kingdoms often had to be changed anyway to suit the myth-maker.[20]

Thus, it was the Roman historians and poets of the first centuries B.C. and A.D. who created the colorful Roman mythology we enjoy today.

1

THE CAPITOLINE TRIAD:

JUPITER, JUNO, AND MINERVA

INTRODUCTION

Even after the Etruscans began to regulate religious practices and took on the role of religious advisers during the seventh century B.C., the Roman people continued to worship their early deities. Roman deities gradually became magnified, however, and many of them began to resemble Etruscan and Greek gods and goddesses. For example, Jupiter (who had been neither godlike nor human but an old stone called Jupiter Lapis) eventually acquired the mythology associated with the Greek god Zeus, king of the gods. Juno, who had been the goddess who presided over everything associated with women, became associated with Hera, queen of the goddesses and wife of Zeus. Minerva, who had been the goddess of activities involving mental skills, became identified with Athena, Greek goddess of wisdom and power.[1]

After Jupiter, Juno, and Minerva began to assume a supreme place in Roman religion, the first Etruscan king, Tarquinius Priscus (616–578 B.C.), built a temple on the Capitoline Hill in their honor. Known as the Capitoline Triad, Jupiter, Juno, and Minerva represented the cornerstone of religious worship. Tarquinius Priscus committed a great deal of money and public works efforts to the building of the temple, but it was never finished during his reign. Many years later, during the sixth century, his grandson Tarquinius Superbus, or Tarquin the Proud, finally finished building the temple. But, like his grandfather, Tarquinius Superbus also spent too much money on its construction. His excesses angered the leading aristocratic families of Rome who had been engaged in a power struggle with the king for some time. The Romans eventually revolted, and the king was overthrown in 510 B.C. before he could dedicate the temple.

The Romans took back their city after Tarquin the Proud was overthrown and arranged their own ceremonies for the dedication of the temple. During the ceremonies, the traditional sacrifice of a live sheep or ox was offered up to Jupiter. The entire ceremony was designed to remind the Roman people that Jupiter was indeed the source of Roman grandness and glory.

Absent in these early ceremonies, however, had been the two goddesses Juno and Minerva, who shared the temple with Jupiter. All the proceedings that went along with the annual ceremonies had been dedicated and addressed to Jupiter, even though the goddesses were part of the Triad. After Augustus became emperor in 27 B.C., however, Juno and Minerva were included in the annual ceremonies and were no longer treated as Jupiter's guests.[2]

THE CAPITOLINE TRIAD: JUPITER, JUNO, AND MINERVA

Jupiter

Jupiter's humble beginnings as sky god and chief god of the Latins can be traced to the region of Italy first settled by early Romans. Some early flint stones were preserved in the Capitol, where he was worshipped as Jupiter Feretrius, "The Oldest."[3]

Jupiter's greatest influence as sky god was through his omens of thunder and lightning. He caused rain to fall on the farms and vineyards of the land and kept the crops well-watered. By the middle of the third century B.C., Jupiter had become the prime protector of Rome and was called Jupiter Optimus ("The Best") Maximus ("The Greatest"). With such an all-encompassing title, Jupiter began to assume a variety of roles that were important to a rising class of educated and wealthy Romans.

The business of governing the people involved the implementation of Roman laws, and Jupiter became, in addition to his agricultural roles, guardian of the law, protector of justice and virtue, and defender of truth. He was known to hand out harsh punishment to perjurers. He was the god upon whom the most solemn oaths were sworn, and he became identified with the goddess of good faith, Fides.[4]

In the first century B.C., the Roman poet Ovid

composed a lyrical version of the Roman calendar called *Fasti*. In this poem, Ovid created mythological stories about Jupiter and King Numa Pompilius, using events that had happened much later than Numa's reign around 700 B.C.

One myth claimed that Jupiter gave King Numa instructions for performing ritual purification and cleansing after lightning struck by sacrificing onions, hair, and fish instead of humans. Another myth alleged that Jupiter had caused a shield, or ancile, to fall from the sky as his gift to King Numa. The king was so delighted with his gift from Jupiter that he had eleven copies of the figure-eight-shaped shield made and locked away in the office of the chief priest for safekeeping. The king claimed that Jupiter's ancile gave him the right to exercise his power over other communities.[4]

Jupiter, by his supreme rank and power, was the sovereign god of the Romans. He was always listed first among the gods or priests, and his symbol was a scepter, the Roman symbol of power. It is no wonder, then, that Jupiter eventually assumed the attributes of Zeus, the supreme god of the Greeks. Just as Zeus was ruler of the Greek pantheon (their collection of gods and goddesses), Jupiter was ruler of the Roman pantheon. Legend credits Jupiter with having granted Neptune dominion over the sea and Pluto dominion over the Underworld.[5]

Juno

The second deity in the Capitoline Triad, Juno, was an early Italian goddess who presided over everything associated with women, especially marriage and childbirth. Juno was protector of women, and she was worshipped under several different names. She presided over marriages as Juno Pronuba, aided women in childbirth as Juno Lucina, and was the special counselor and protector of the Roman state as Juno Regina.

After the Romans created their own pantheon of gods and goddesses, Juno became queen of the goddesses, the female counterpart of Jupiter. In March, when all nature was being renewed, Juno (goddess of marriage and childbirth) was honored during the festival known as Matronalia.[6] Although the festival was celebrated in early spring, the month of June is named after Juno, and it is today considered by many people to be the perfect time of year to be married.

Juno was also worshipped in the temple *ad Monetam* next to the Roman mint on Capitoline Hill. In this temple, she was known as Juno Moneta ("Adviser"). After the Etruscan city Veii was conquered in 396 B.C., Juno Regina (Queen Juno) was invited to come to Rome. By accepting the invitation, it is believed she came willingly and thus deprived the Etruscans of her protection. Under the influence of the Greeks, Juno became the wife and sister of Jupiter, and her greatest power and mythology came from Hera, her Greek counterpart.[7]

Minerva

Minerva, introduced to the Romans by the Etruscans in the late eighth or early seventh century b.c., was the third member of the Capitoline Triad. The Romans regarded her as the goddess of all activities involving mental skill. She was also known as the goddess of war, crafts, and science. After Minerva became associated with the Greek goddess Athena, she acquired a more expanded mythology. One story tells that Minerva sprang from the head of Jupiter fully clothed in armor and ready for battle. Minerva was credited with having invented the trumpet and flute, as well as utensils and tools. She was worshipped as goddess of the arts of women, which included the arts of cooking and weaving.[8]

Although Minerva was vain, she did not take lovers. She was known to be quite modest, and was said to have blinded a man who happened to have witnessed her bathing in a stream. Minerva's favorite bird was the owl, for which we remember her to this day: The owl remains a symbol of wisdom.

QUESTIONS AND ANSWERS

Q: *Tarquinius Priscus began construction of the temple to Jupiter Optimus Maximus. Who finished it?*

A: His grandson, Tarquin the Proud, finished building the temple, but the Roman people overthrew Tarquin in 510 B.C. before the temple could be dedicated.

Q: *What was the Capitoline Triad?*

A: It was a trinity of deities—Jupiter, Juno, and Minerva—that represented the foundation of Roman religion.

Q: *List three aspects of Roman law that Jupiter influenced.*

A: He was guardian of the law, protector of justice and virtue, and defender of truth.

Q: *What three items did the Romans believe Jupiter told King Numa to use for sacrifices after lightning struck?*

A: He told him to substitute onions, hair, and fish for human sacrifices.

Q: *At what time of year was Juno's festival, Matronalia, celebrated? What month was named after this goddess?*

A: The festival was held in March, but the month of June is named after the goddess.

Q: *List four items associated with Minerva.*

A: Utensils, tools, the trumpet, and the flute are all associated with the goddess Minerva.

Q: *Jupiter, Juno, and Minerva were identified with which of the Greek gods and goddesses?*

A: Jupiter was identified with Zeus, king of the gods. Juno was identified with Hera, the wife of Zeus and queen of the goddesses. Minerva was identified with Athena, goddess of wisdom and power.

EXPERT COMMENTARY

Jupiter was grouped with Mars and Quirinus in an early triad of gods. However, the Capitoline Triad, in which his consorts were Juno and Minerva, was the most important grouping. Stewart Perowne describes the significance of the Capitoline Triad:

> This later triad [Jupiter, Juno, and Minerva] was the principal focus of Roman veneration. The Roman Capitol was its dwelling-place. In the most high and palmy state of Rome, when countless cities owned her sway, it was the first care of a city's architect to raise a capitol analogous to that of Rome, and on it to install the three deities, with Jupiter enthroned in the midst.[9]

Mark P. O. Morford and Mark J. Lenardon in *Classical Mythology* described the ancile that Jupiter caused to fall from the sky and the ceremonies surrounding its use as follows:

> This *ancile* was of the archaic figure-eight shape; since it was a talisman [a small object kept or worn for its magical power] of Roman power, Numa had eleven others made exactly like it, so that it would be hard to steal the genuine *ancile*. The twelve ancilia were kept in the Regia (the office of the Pontifex Maximus, the official head of the hierarchy of the state religion), and were used by the priests of Mars, the Salii, in the sacred war dance which they performed each spring. As they danced, they sang an ancient hymn containing the words *mamuri veturi*, whose meaning had long since been forgotten. According to tradition, the craftsman who made the eleven false "ancilia" was named Mamurius, who asked for his name to be included in the hymn as a reward.[10]

Minerva is an example of a goddess whose origins were Etruscan. She eventually became part of the Roman Capitoline Triad and acquired the mythology of the Greek goddess Athena. According to Jane F. Gardner in *Roman Myths*:

> Minerva was an Italian goddess of handicrafts. For the Romans, she was one of their chief triad of gods, Jupiter, Juno and Minerva, with a temple on the Capitol. The temple and its triad came to symbolise being Roman, and were reduplicated all over the Roman empire. The Romans themselves believed that it had been instituted, c. 509 B.C., by Rome's last king, Tarquin the Proud. His father had come from Etruria, which may tell us something about Minerva's origins, while her elevation to a senior position, like Athena, perhaps reflects the influence of Greek culture on the Etruscans already at that period.[11]

2

ROMAN DEITIES:

MARS, VENUS, AND APOLLO

INTRODUCTION

As the father of twin sons, Romulus and Remus, Mars became one of the immortal ancestors of the Roman people.[1] He gained popularity after the myth about the founding of Rome by Romulus became widely known.

Venus' status also became important to the Roman people because she was the mother of Aeneas, who founded Lavinium. Originally, Venus was patroness of gardens and vineyards and was worshipped as goddess of love and beauty. Her exalted position as goddess of motherhood and marriage was initiated by Julius Caesar, who built a temple for her in 46 B.C. and claimed the goddess as one of his ancestors.[2]

Although most of the gods and goddesses adopted by the Romans from the Greeks were given Latin names, Apollo was one of the few gods who was "Apollo" to both the Greeks and the Romans. The Romans worshipped him as god of power and healing prophecies—the god who taught them about medicine. Legends tell of Apollo's birth in Asia Minor in present-day Turkey, the birthplace of Aeneas. Because the Romans believed that their ancestors came from Asia Minor, Apollo's origins made him important to the Romans.

Like the Greeks, the Romans began to consult the oracles of Apollo at a temple in Delphi situated on the spur of Mount Parnassus in southern Greece. They believed that Apollo could foretell the future and that his oracle, or prophecy, could be obtained from an old priestess who kept watch over his temple there. Romans sought Apollo's advice during the many wars they fought to control their empire. Other oracles of Apollo existed on the island of

Delos; in other parts of Greece; and in Anatolia, in present-day Turkey. During Aeneas' journey in search of the Trojans' ancestral homeland, he sought the advice of a priestess who lived in a cave beneath Apollo's temple on Delos. The oracle at Delphi, however, was considered the most important of them all.[3]

ROMAN DEITIES: MARS, VENUS, AND APOLLO

Mars

By the fourth century B.C., Mars, the Roman god of agriculture, had already assumed the form and shape of a warrior. He was portrayed wearing armor and a crested helmet and carrying a shield. In preparation for war, Roman soldiers practiced vigorous drilling exercises on the Campus Martius, or "field of Mars," located beyond the city walls next to the Tiber River. Mars was worshipped on the Capitol in a temple that he shared with Jupiter and Quirinus, another god of war. The Roman army would gather at the site of the temple Mars Gradvisu before leaving for war. Still another temple—one that he shared with Venus—was built on the Forum Augustus. This temple was known as Mars Ultor ("The Avenger").

There were several festivals held in honor of Mars. The most notable festival was the Armilustrium, which was celebrated in October when the military weapons of the soldiers were ritually purified and then stored away for winter. Wars were often begun or continued in spring; thus, the month of March (Martius) was named after the god Mars.

Mars became identified with Ares, the Greek god of war. Unlike Mars, however, Ares was cruel and vain. Mars

was said to have been the husband of Bellona, a serpent-haired goddess who represented conflict as well as peace. Bellona was sometimes described as being the feminine side of Mars.

Venus

After the Romans began to identify Venus with Aphrodite, the Greek goddess of love, Venus' mythology became much the same as Aphrodite's. She was believed by some to be the daughter of Jupiter, and by others to have sprung from the foam of the sea. As the daughter of Jupiter, she was protected by her father, who believed all the gods wanted to take her hand in marriage. So Jupiter arranged for his daughter to marry Vulcan, the god of volcanic fire, who was the most steady and reliable of the gods—and one of the ugliest.[3]

There are two legends associated with the god Vulcan. The first is that he was born weak and crippled, and that his mother, Juno, unable to look at him, threw him off Mount Olympus, the legendary home of the Greek gods. Seven days later, Vulcan landed in the sea, where he was rescued by nymphs. They took him to the island of Lemnos in the northern Aegean and cared for him. The second legend claims that Vulcan took his mother Juno's side during a family argument and that his father, Jupiter, threw him off Mount Olympus. In this version, too, Vulcan fell for seven days, but this time he landed directly on the island of Lemnos.

Regardless of Vulcan's beginnings, he was thrilled to have been given Venus' hand in marriage. Vulcan wanted so much to please his new wife that he fashioned beautiful gold jewelry for her and even made her a finely woven gold girdle to wrap around her thin young waist. The gold girdle, however, only made Venus more irresistible to men.

Vulcan became perpetually jealous of his beautiful wife and was always accusing her of adulterous affairs. His jealousy was not unfounded. Venus spent a great deal of time with other men, and her favorite lover was the god Mars. One day, Vulcan sneaked up on his wife, who was lying in the arms of Mars, and threw a finely woven net over them so that they could not get free. The angry husband took the illicit lovers to the Olympian gods and asked that they be punished for their affair. The gods, however, laughed at the sight of the embarrassed couple wrapped in each other's arms and set them free.

Paris, a Trojan prince, awarded Venus a golden apple,

the prize for the most beautiful goddess. Jupiter had been asked to choose the most beautiful goddess from among Juno, Minerva, and Venus, but he had feared the wrath of the losers. So, he asked the mortal Paris to give the award.

Paris had a difficult time trying to decide among the goddesses until, finally, they volunteered to help him. Each goddess agreed to offer him a gift, and the gift of his choice would name the winner. Minerva offered him great wisdom and great luck in war. Juno offered him all of Asia and great power. Venus offered to give him the most beautiful woman in the world.

Because Paris adored beautiful women, he chose

Venus' gift and asked for Helen, wife of King Menelaus of Greece. Venus helped Paris abduct Helen from Sparta, and the Greek world went to war over the incident—it caused the Trojan War.[4]

Apollo

Apollo was a god of many things and was one of the most worshipped of the Greek and Roman gods. He was god of the shepherds, god of light and truth, god of healing, god of prophecy, god of music, and god of archery. His most important daily task was to harness his four horses to his chariot and drive the sun across the sky.

Apollo was the son of Jupiter and the goddess Latona, known as the "hidden one." Apollo's twin sister was the goddess Diana. Apollo and Diana were very protective of their mother and quick to defend her. One day, Queen Niobe of Thebes, the principal city in Boeotia, an early Greek territory, bragged to Latona that she was a superior woman because she had given birth to fourteen children and Latona had only given birth to twins. Angered by the queen's smugness, Apollo and Diana decided to make the queen childless so that their own mother would be the better woman. The queen had seven boys and seven girls—so Apollo killed the boys, and Diana killed the girls.

Although Apollo was known to have had many romances, some legends say that he never married. He was, however, one of the first gods to fall in love with a member of the same sex—a handsome Spartan prince named Hyacinthus, who was also loved by Favonius, god of the west wind. Hyacinthus returned Apollo's love, but he would not return the affection of Favonius. So one day when Apollo and Hyacinthus were out in a field throwing the discus, Favonius blew the discus toward Hyacinthus' head. It struck the young prince in the skull and killed him.

In the pool of blood that formed beside his head, Apollo made a flower spring forth from the earth: a hyacinth.

Other legends claimed that Apollo loved a beautiful young woman named Daphne, who would not return his love. Daphne, in fact, became irritated by the god's persistent attentions. When Apollo refused to leave her alone, she asked her father, the river god Peneus, for help. Because water gods always had the power of transformation, Peneus transformed his daughter into a beautiful laurel tree. Apollo then claimed the laurel tree as his own, and laurel leaves became his symbol.

According to another legend, Apollo eventually married a nymph named Larissa. The couple was very happy, and Apollo believed that, at last, he had found true love. But one day his favorite bird, the crow (who, at that time, had pure white feathers), came to him and told him that his beautiful wife had been unfaithful to him. Apollo flew into a rage and shot Larissa with one of his sharp arrows. Although he had not intended to kill her, Larissa was fatally injured and Apollo could not make her return to life. Angry that he had lost the woman he loved, Apollo turned on the crow that had delivered the news and changed his white feathers into black. Then, he forbade the crow to ever fly among other birds.[5]

Apollo's symbols are a lyre, which represents harmony, and a bow, which represents his power to destroy. Apollo was known to be kind and forgiving, but mean and vicious, as well.

QUESTIONS AND ANSWERS

Q: *Was Apollo a Greek or Roman god?*

A: Apollo was initially a Greek god who was basically adopted as a Roman god. "Apollo" is the name used by both the Greeks and the Romans.

Q: *Name three places where people went to learn of the oracles of Apollo.*

A: They went to Delphi in Greece, Anatolia in present-day Turkey, and the island of Delos in the Aegean Sea.

Q: *Mars was the Roman god of agriculture. With what Greek god did he become associated?*

A: Mars later became associated with Ares, the Greek god of war.

Q: *Venus was the Roman patroness of gardens and vineyards. With what Greek goddess did she become associated?*

A: Venus acquired the mythology of Aphrodite, the Greek goddess of love and beauty.

Q: *How did Apollo and his sister, Diana, protect their mother?*

A: They murdered the fourteen children of Queen Niobe of Thebes because she had bragged that, because she had more children, she was a better woman than their mother. Apollo killed the queen's seven boys and Diana killed her seven girls.

Q: *Who were Apollo's lovers?*

A: He loved a Spartan prince named Hyacinthus, a young woman named Daphne, and a nymph named Larissa.

Q: *Why is the month of March associated with the god Mars?*

A: Spring was the time of year when wars began or were continued.

Q: *Describe the Greek god with whom Mars came to be identified.*

A: He became associated with Ares, the Greek god of war, who was mean and cruel.

Q: *Name the god who won Venus' hand in marriage.*

A: Vulcan, the god of volcanic fire, whom Jupiter believed to be the steadiest and most reliable of the gods.

Q: *Why did Paris award Venus the golden apple, proclaiming her the most beautiful goddess?*

A: Venus promised to give Paris the gift of the world's most beautiful woman if she were awarded the golden apple. She was competing against Juno, queen of the goddesses, and Minerva, goddess of wisdom and war, whose gifts the Prince did not choose to accept.

EXPERT COMMENTARY

The origins of Mars were obscured after his association with Ares, the Greek god of war:

> "Mars was the Roman god of war but he also has agrarian attributes. His festivals fell mostly within the month, which still bears his name. As the 'off-season' for both war and agriculture was the same in antiquity, namely from autumn to spring, his dual role is perfectly logical."[6]

In the "Calendar of Roman Religion," the *Feast of the Tiber* reveals some interesting information about the campus of Mars that was located outside the walls of the city close to the Tiber River:

> One June 7th, the Romans held the games of Tiber on the Campus Martius. As noted elsewhere, the River had received its Roman name from the Alban King Tiberinus [legendary eighth king of Alba Longa] who had drowned in its waters, it having been previously known as Albula [meaning *white*]. Both names make clear the connection to the settlement at Mt. Alba. The color white being an attribute of the goddess Ceres and of divinity in general, the White Mountain and the White River are obviously sacred, and they reinforce the Roman idea that they themselves had a divine source.[7]

Romans did not change the name of the Greek god Apollo after he joined their pantheon of gods. He was known by the same name to both Greeks and Latins, and for good reason:

> [Apollo] arrived as the result of a pestilence, and his temple was dedicated in 431 B.C., two years after the Sibylline books had been consulted . . .
>
> [H]e was never as prominent at Rome as he was in the Greek world. He was worshipped originally as Apollo Medicus (corresponding to his Greek title of Paean, the Healer).[8]

3

AENEAS' JOURNEY TO CRETE

INTRODUCTION

The Aeneid, composed by the Roman poet Virgil (30–19 B.C.), tells of the mythological journey of a young Trojan named Aeneas, who takes his people in search of a new homeland after Troy, an ancient city in northwest Asia Minor, is destroyed by the Greeks in 1250 B.C.[1]

When the Roman people began to read Virgil's epic poem in the first century B.C., they were already familiar with the Etruscan and Greek equivalents of the Roman gods and goddesses. They were also accepting of gods and goddesses who interacted with mortals in their myths. So the unfolding of Aeneas' saga with its interweaving of the actions of mortals and gods and goddesses was not strange, but rather it reinforced the Romans' desire for an exalted heritage. Highlights of Aeneas' journey have been included in this book, and it is hoped that readers will be inspired to read *The Aeneid* and choose their own favorite portions of the poem.

This chapter summarizes Aeneas' journey to Crete and the hardships he and his companions endured during their journey and stay on the island.

Aeneas' Journey to Crete

Aeneas, a young Trojan soldier, had grown up with war. He did not believe that his beloved city of Troy would ever fall to the Greeks. But one night, the ghost of Hector, a dead Trojan hero, appeared to Aeneas as he slept. Hector's ghost warned Aeneas that Troy was doomed and would be overrun by the warring Greek armies the next day. He told Aeneas to gather up the household deities, the Lares and Penates, and lead his people from the burning city.

Alarmed by this strange nocturnal warning, Aeneas awoke, put on his armor, and hurried into the city. Greek soldiers had already stormed the walls and were burning Troy to the ground. Aeneas joined other Trojan soldiers and they fought their way toward King Priam's palace. But they were too late to save the lives of King Priam and his royal Trojan family. Outside the king's chamber, Aeneas and his men heard King Priam bellowing at Greek soldiers for murdering his son, Polites. After the boy was killed, King Priam himself was murdered.

Aeneas was terrified. He feared the same fate might soon befall his own family, so he left the palace and ran all the way home. However, Aeneas need not have feared. Unbeknownst to him, his mother, the goddess Venus, was watching and protecting them so that no harm would befall his family.

When Aeneas entered his house, his father (Anchises), his son (Ascanius), and his wife (Creüsa), were seated around a small wooden table drinking warm milk and eating honey-coated bread, completely unaware of what was happening in their city. Aeneas explained to them that Greek soldiers had stormed the city and the family must leave immediately. However, the crippled Anchises refused to go. Aeneas had to plead with his father to join them, stating that they would not leave without him.

Confused and bewildered, Anchises prayed out loud to Jupiter for guidance. Jupiter responded by sending down an omen in the form of a bolt of lightning and a loud crack of thunder. Anchises interpreted these signs from Jupiter to mean that he should leave Troy with Aeneas and his family. As Anchises prepared to go, he gathered up the Penates and the Lares to take along with them.

Aeneas gently hoisted his father onto his broad shoulders and took the hand of little Ascanius. He brushed a kiss against Creüsa's cheek and asked that she follow close behind them. Then Aeneas led his family from their safe home, traveling by way of dark alleyways, cautious to avoid the Greek soldiers. His long strides made it difficult for his son and wife to keep up, and they quickly became tired. When they were finally outside the gates of the city, Aeneas set his father down on the ground and released his son's hand. But when he turned around, Creüsa was no longer with them. Aeneas realized he had not looked behind him to see if she had been following. Panicked that he had walked too fast and that Greek soldiers may have ambushed her, Aeneas ran at breakneck speed back into the burning city.

Meanwhile, the soldiers had burned Aeneas' house and many of the nearby homes to the ground. As Aeneas stared into the empty ruins, he saw someone move toward him. He suddenly realized it was Creüsa and ran toward her. But when he reached out to hold his wife in his arms, he could gather only the smoky air of her ghost. But Creüsa's voice was reassuring, and she told her husband that it was the will of the gods that she remain behind. She warned him that the gods had predicted a long and dangerous journey ahead for the Trojan people. Aeneas reached out twice more to wrap his arms around his beloved wife, but each time he could feel only Creüsa's ghost. He turned and ran back to his son and father, who had been joined by other Trojans and were waiting for him to lead them away.

Aeneas and the Trojans who had escaped the destruction of their city worked diligently for many months to build enough wooden ships to carry them across the sea in search of a new homeland. The ships they built had decks below to accommodate passengers; middle decks filled with benches to hold the oarsmen, whose long oars extended through holes in the sides of the ships; and top decks with great tall sails in the center.

When at last the ships were ready and loaded with provisions, the fleet set sail north toward Thrace, a country known to be an ally of the Trojans. Aeneas wished to visit Polydorus, King Priam's youngest son, who had been sent there for safekeeping. Once Aeneas and his people were safely ashore in Thrace, Aeneas built the customary sacrificial altar to honor the gods and goddesses of the land. But when he uprooted some myrtle to decorate the altar, blood dripped from its leaves and a muffled sob burst forth from the earth. The voice belonged to young Polydorus, who had been killed by the Thracians after they had changed their alliance with the Trojans to one with the Greeks.

Aeneas was saddened by the loss of yet another

member of the royal family. He and his people held a proper funeral for Polydorus before leaving Thrace. The Trojan women let down their hair, recited mournful prayers, and put to rest the spirit of the young prince.

Aeneas, unable to decide in which direction they must sail to find their ancestral homeland, steered the fleet to Delos, a small Greek island in the Aegean Sea. The god Apollo had been born on this island, and Aeneas decided to consult with a priestess who lived there in a cave beneath Apollo's temple. She would relay Apollo's prophecy, or oracle, to those who came for advice. Aeneas found the priestess and asked:

Whom should we follow? Or by what sea way
Dost thou direct us? Where may we settle now?
Father, grant us a sign, enter our hearts![2]

The oracle answered and advised the Trojans to seek the land from which they first sprang. Aeneas did not understand what the oracle meant, so he consulted his father. Anchises remembered a legend about one of Troy's founders who came from Crete, a very large island in the Mediterranean Sea. The old man convinced his son that Apollo's oracle had meant that they should settle on the island of Crete. Thus, having solved the mystery of the oracle, Aeneas offered prayers of thanks to Apollo and set sail.

Situated halfway between Asia Minor and the Greek mainland, Crete appeared to be a most suitable site for the Trojans. After anchoring, the Trojans celebrated the founding of their new homeland. Their spirits were high, and everyone worked hard to build a new life on the island. Men and women plowed the island's fertile fields, planted crops of barley and millet, and tended the fruit and olive trees that grew generously all over the island. Acneas

offered his people hope by parceling out individual plots of land and by establishing a set of laws designed to guide them. But their happiness was short-lived. Within a year, a devastating plague struck the island and killed plants, animals, and people. The Trojans could not understand why the gods were so angry with them.

Then one night, Penates and the Lares (the Trojan household gods that had been with Aeneas since he left Troy) appeared. They chorused:

> *Keep up the long toil of your flight. Your settlement*
> *Must be changed. This coast is not the one*
> *Apollo of Delos urged you toward, nor did he*
> *Bid you stay on Crete. There is a country,*
> *Hesperia, as the Greeks have named it—ancient,*
> *Full of man-power in war and fruitful earth...*[3]

The following morning, Aeneas told his people about his vision, and he encouraged them to remain hopeful. With such positive guidance, the Trojans happily packed up and left the island and set out for Hesperia, the land the Greeks called Italy.

QUESTIONS AND ANSWERS

Q: *How did Aeneas learn that Troy was going to be taken by the Greeks?*

A: The ghost of Hector, a dead Trojan hero, came to him in the night and told him to lead his people from the doomed city of Troy.

Q: *Who was Aeneas' mother?*

A: Venus, goddess of love.

Q: *What gods and/or goddesses played a part in Aeneas' journey to Crete?*

A: Venus, Aeneas' immortal mother and goddess of love; Jupiter, chief god of the Romans; and Apollo, god of prophecy.

Q: *What is the role of the gods in the Trojans' escape from Troy and their journey to Crete?*

A: Venus watched over Aeneas' family during the burning of Troy; Jupiter, father of the gods, sent a sign telling Anchises to leave Troy with his son; and Apollo, god of prophecy, delivered an oracle to Aeneas on the island of Delos.

Q: *Why did the Trojans believe Crete was their ancestral homeland?*

A: Long ago, the Trojans were believed to have come from Crete, and Anchises, Aeneas' father, interpreted Apollo's oracle to mean they should settle there.

Q: *Why did the settlement on Crete fail?*

A: The island was devastated by a great plague.

Q: *Who were the deities that appeared to Aeneas to tell him that Apollo did not mean for him to settle in Crete, and what did they say?*

A: The household deities, the Penates and the Lares, appeared to Aeneas with veils over their heads. They said that Apollo's oracle meant they should settle in Hesperia, the land the Greeks called Italy.

EXPERT COMMENTARY

Scholars suggest that Virgil helped form the image of Aeneas as pious, meaning that he was obedient to the will of the gods, his family, and country:

> This close connection between the ancestral gods and the pietas [piety] of the hero is important for an understanding of the meaning of pietas in Italy. We can be sure that pietas in the late sixth and early fifth centuries B.C., which is the time of the first representations of Aeneas on Italian soil, did not have some vastly extended meaning which it had at the time of Augustus and Virgil, when it had been the programmatic quality of the first citizen, Augustus, and the ideal Roman citizen Aeneas.[4]
>
> Virgil's portrayal of Aeneas, therefore, has its roots in Italy. It is no coincidence that the Roman poet was the first and only writer who made Italy the native land of Aeneas. The poet gave this pietas infinitely more connotation than it had originally and thus was able to adapt a hero whose character had been rather contradictory to his own purposes.[5]

Virgil wrote *The Aeneid* at the request of Augustus, so it is not surprising that much of the story reflects well on the emperor. It is quite probable that Virgil would have readily admitted that *The Aeneid* was propaganda. And propaganda was, in this case, a distortion of the truth to make Augustus appear great. The point was to show a connection between the "pious Aeneas" (and his immortal ancestry) and Augustus.[6]

4

AENEAS MEETS DIDO

INTRODUCTION

After the Trojans learned that Apollo's oracle at Delos did not mean they should settle on the island of Crete, they were happy to continue their quest for a new homeland. Still unaware that Venus had been guiding them along the way, the Trojans set out. Little did they dream that their journey would be visited, guided, and harassed by both gods and goddesses.

Juno, still angry with the Trojans because Paris had given the golden apple for most beautiful goddess to Venus, would try to get even with the Trojans—and in particular, with Venus. The scheming of Juno and Venus began shortly after the Trojan fleet left Crete and continued long after the Trojans reached the magnificent port city of Carthage.

In Carthage, the Trojans met the lovely Queen Dido, a beautiful young woman who had escaped her home in Tyre, on the present-day coast of Lebanon, after her husband had killed her brother. Juno schemed to get Aeneas and Dido married so that the Trojans would not leave Carthage and build a rival city, and Venus schemed to get them married so that Dido would not harm the Trojans. Both Juno and Venus enlisted the gods in their plans.

AENEAS MEETS DIDO

Although sickness and loss had weakened their bodies, the Trojans' spirits were high when they left Crete. They believed that they would soon find their true homeland. The land that Apollo had called Hesperia, however, continued to elude them. Scarcely a few miles out at sea, a vicious storm tossed the Trojans onto another island, which was inhabited by the Harpies, a group of ugly winged creatures with women's faces. Before Aeneas and his people could get away from the island, the Harpies had stolen their food and attacked them. Celaeno, a prophetic Harpy, told them that she had received an oracle from Apollo that foretold of much hardship ahead for the Trojans. She said Apollo predicted that hunger would cause them to eat their tables when they finally found Hesperia.

Disgusted by the sight of the ugly bird-women and confused by Apollo's oracle, the Trojans packed up and left the island in a hurry. They enjoyed a well-deserved rest at Actium on the western coast of Greece, where they played games and socialized for many months. Then, they sailed farther up the coast to Buthrotum, where Aeneas consulted with Helenus, an exiled Trojan ruler. Helenus told the Trojans that the land the Greeks called Hesperia was still a long way off. He also warned them that they should not sail through the strait between Italy and Sicily, but must take the long way around Sicily to avoid Scylla and Charybdis, the two terrible monsters that guarded the strait. Scylla had six heads and used them to snatch men from ships that came too close to the Italian shore. Charybdis, a whirlpool, sucked the ships down as they tried to escape from Scylla.

With this warning in mind, the Trojan fleet set out for the Italian peninsula and sailed safely around the coast of Sicily, where the men went ashore. Suddenly, a giant one-eyed creature appeared and began to move down the

mountain toward them. Having heard horrible stories about the Cyclopes, the Trojan men fled back to their ship. One Cyclops, who had recently been blinded, waded out into the water and stumbled in the direction of the escaping ship. The sight of the fearsome creature frightened the Trojans. They quickly pulled in their anchor, raised their sails, and rowed out to sea.

After escaping from the Cyclops, the Trojans stopped to rest at Drepanum, on the northwestern end of the island of Sicily. There, Anchises died. The oracle had not foretold

this horrible tragedy, and Aeneas became spiritless and depressed at the loss of his beloved father.

After a prolonged period of mourning, Aeneas pulled himself together and ordered the ships to set a course north through the Tyrrhenian Sea. Aeneas' fleet was suddenly faced with the treachery of Juno, who realized that the Trojans might actually succeed in finding their way to Italy. To deter the Trojans, Juno concocted a scheme with Aeolus, god of the wind, to create a great storm at sea and drown the fleet. Aeolus' breath tossed the ships from side to side and forward and backward creating great waves that hit the Trojan ships from all directions. Women and children screamed in fear as the waves washed men and equipment overboard. The helmsmen were unable to hold a course, and for the first time since leaving Troy, Aeneas feared for his life.

Then, just when survival seemed unlikely and the Trojans prepared to die at sea, the wind ceased. Neptune, god of the sea and an ally of the Trojans, awoke from his sleep. He scolded Aeolus for causing a storm without his permission, then gently guided the fleet to a quiet harbor along the northern coast of Africa. After the ships had dropped anchor, Aeneas helped carry the women and children to shore. He covered their shivering bodies with dry grain sacks and assured them that they would indeed find their ancestral homeland and should not lose hope.

While the Trojans were recovering from their terrible ordeal at sea, Venus visited with Juno's husband, Jupiter. Venus reminded him that he once had promised her that he would guide Aeneas to Italy. Jupiter assured her that he had not forgotten this promise:

> *In Italy he will fight a massive war,*
> *Beat down fierce armies, then for the people there*
> *Establish city walls and a way of life.*[1]

In the meantime, Aeneas and his best friend, Achates, set off on foot to explore the shores of northern Africa. Along the way, they stopped and conversed with a young huntress—Aeneas' immortal mother, Venus, in disguise. Venus feared that the Carthaginians would harm her son and his friend, so she enveloped them an invisible cloud before saying goodbye. Soon, Aeneas and Achates reached the city of Carthage and came to a temple dedicated to Juno, which was set off in a dense olive grove. Standing beside the door of the temple, the men heard Queen Dido offering advice and counsel to three Trojan men, whom Aeneas believed had been lost at sea. The men were telling about their perilous journey from Troy, but before they could finish, Dido interrupted and asked if she could meet their leader. Aeneas and Achates wasted no time slipping from beneath their invisible cloud. When Aeneas stepped forward and admitted that he was the leader of the Trojan people, the queen smiled warmly and asked that he finish telling the tale at a banquet that she would give in his honor. Aeneas accepted the invitation and asked if he could bring along his young son, Ascanius. The queen agreed.

On the evening of the palace banquet, Venus sent her immortal son, Cupid, the god of love, to the palace disguised as Ascanius. She believed that Dido would not harm Aeneas if the queen fell in love with him. So according to his mother's instructions, Cupid sat on Dido's lap and cast his spell. While Aeneas entertained Queen Dido's dinner guests with the long saga of the Trojans' journey to Carthage, Cupid made Dido fall helplessly in love with the young Trojan.

That night, Dido confessed to her sister Anna that she had fallen in love with Aeneas. Now she had a dilemma. She could no longer honor the vow she had taken to remain faithful to her dead husband. Anna reminded Dido that she had been a widow long enough and suggested that the city of Carthage might benefit from the presence of the Trojans, who would discourage invasions of other, more warlike foreigners.

From then on, Dido was consumed by Cupid's spell and her love for Aeneas. She could not get Aeneas out of her mind, much less her heart, and she soon began to neglect the business of building her city. Likewise, Aeneas was captivated by Dido's beauty and charm and visited her every evening. Together these lovers roamed Carthage's narrow winding streets lined with tall, closely packed houses, and they often went to visit the harbor.

Aeneas was impressed with the city's modern double-ringed harbor. The outer harbor accommodated trading ships. The inner harbor, a large, rounded area lined with hundreds of sheds, protected Dido's warships.

Soon, the couple was spending so much time together that Dido had completely neglected her royal duties. Juno decided that perhaps Dido might be more inclined to concentrate on building and governing her city if she and Aeneas were married. Marriage would also mean that Aeneas would remain in Carthage. So one day, while Dido and Aeneas were out riding, Juno caused a violent thunderstorm. The weather was so inclement that the couple had to seek shelter in a small cave. When the storm cleared, Aeneas and Dido left the cave. Juno wasted no time exposing their secret affair.

The rumor spread quickly throughout the city and among the gods, and when Jupiter heard the story, he became alarmed. Quickly, Jupiter summoned Mercury, the messenger god, and instructed him to visit the lovesick Trojan leader to remind him that he had an obligation to the gods and to his people to lead the Trojans to a new homeland. Mercury also reminded Aeneas that his young son, Ascanius, would never lay claim to land of his own if the Trojans remained forever in Carthage.

Finally, Aeneas understood the consequences of his actions. He agreed with Mercury that the Trojans must leave Carthage, but the decision to leave the woman he loved broke his heart. Still, Aeneas told his men to prepare to set sail the following morning. But the young lover, lacking the courage to break the news to Dido, made his preparations in secret.

The queen soon learned the truth, and she hurried off to confront her lover:

> *You even hoped to keep me in the dark*
> *As to this outrage, did you, two-faced man,*
> *And slip away in silence? Can our love*
> *Not hold you, can the pledge we gave not hold you,*
> *Can Dido not, now sure to die in pain?*[2]

Aeneas tried to make the beautiful queen understand that the decision to leave Carthage had not been his own, but had been decreed by the gods. He assured her that he loved her but explained that his love for the gods, his people, the memory of his dead father, and his son's future, were even more important.

Aeneas' determination to leave and his explanations only made Dido angrier. She warned him that if he left, she would haunt him for the rest of his life.

> *I hope and pray that on some grinding reef*
> *Midway at sea you'll drink your punishment*
> *And call and call on Dido's name!*
> *From far away I shall come after you*
> *With my black fires, and when cold death has parted*
> *Body from soul I shall be everywhere*
> *A shade to haunt you! You will pay for this.*[3]

That night, Aeneas tossed restlessly in his sleep until Mercury awakened him to warn him of the queen's plan to burn his entire fleet in the morning. Mercury advised Aeneas to leave Carthage right away under cover of darkness. Always respectful of Mercury's warnings, Aeneas awoke his people and told them to prepare for immediate departure. Then, in the still of a dark moonless night, the fleet sailed quietly out of the harbor.

The following morning, Dido saw from her window the sails of the Trojan ships far off in the distance. Her chance to burn the fleet had been lost, and the ships were already too far out at sea for her ships to take pursuit. Angrier than she had ever been, Dido called out to the gods to hear her vengeful prophecy:

> *Let him see the unmerited deaths of those*
> *Around and with him, and accepting peace*
> *On unjust terms, let him not, even so,*
> *Enjoy his kingdom or the life he longs for,*
> *But fall in battle before his time and lie*
> *Unburied on the sand! This I implore,*
> *This is my last cry, as my last blood flows.*
> *Then, O my Tyrians, besiege with hate*
> *His progeny and all his race to come:*
> *Make this offering to my dust. No love,*
> *No pact must be between our peoples; No,*
> *But rise up from my bones, avenging spirit!*[4]

After Aeneas left Carthage, the beautiful Dido became overwhelmed with despair. She had broken her vows to her dead husband after she had fallen in love with Aeneas, and now she had lost her self-respect because Aeneas had rejected her. Dido called her sister Anna to her side and asked that she have built a funeral pyre upon which the queen would burn everything that Aeneas had left behind him, including their love.

As the funeral pyre was being built, Dido secretly watched from her window. When it was completed, she rushed out into the courtyard carrying a long shining sword—a gift from Aeneas—and climbed onto the pyre. Then before her sister or attendants could stop her, Queen Dido plunged the sword into her own chest. As Anna approached, the life began to leave Dido's body. The queen struggled to raise herself on one elbow:

> *"I die unavenged," she said,"but let me die.*
> *This way, this way, a blessed relief to go*
> *Into the undergloom. Let the cold Trojan,*
> *Far at sea, drink in this conflagration [fire]*
> *And take with him the omen of my death!"*[5]

Anna took the dying queen in her arms and sobbed helplessly.

> *It came to this, then, sister? You deceived me?*
> *The pyre meant this, altars and fires meant this?*
> *What shall I mourn first, being abandoned? Did you*
> *Scorn your sister's company in death?*
> *You should have called me out to the same fate!*[6]

Juno looked down on the dying queen and suffered a brief moment of regret. Her failed scheme had caused Dido to suffer more than the goddess had intended. Then, Juno took pity on the young queen and sent a messenger to free Dido's soul from her dying body.

QUESTIONS AND ANSWERS

Q: *What part does Aeolus, god of wind, play in this story?*

A: Aeolus agrees to Juno's plan to keep the Trojans from reaching Italy. He creates a great storm at sea in an effort to drown the Trojan fleet.

Q: *Who is Jupiter? Is he a friend or foe of the Trojans?*

A: Jupiter, king of the gods and the husband of Juno, is a friend of the Trojans.

Q: *Why does Juno, queen of the gods, hate the Trojans?*

A: Juno hates the Trojans because Paris, a Trojan prince, did not award her the golden apple as prize for being the most beautiful goddess. Paris awarded it, instead, to Venus.

Q: *Why did Venus and Juno both want Aeneas and Dido to fall in love?*

A: Venus believed that marriage would protect her son from any harm Dido might do to him. Juno wanted to keep Aeneas in Carthage so that he would never build a rival city in Italy.

Q: *Does Dido appear to be a victim or a villain?*

A: Both. Dido schemed to get Aeneas to stay in Carthage because she loved him, but she was also a victim of Juno's scheming. Juno's failed plot to have Aeneas and Dido married so that the Trojans would never build a rival city caused the queen to kill herself.

Q: *What is Aeneas' conflict in leaving Dido and Carthage?*

A: He must choose between duty and desire. His duty is

to take his people to Italy, but he desires to stay with the beautiful queen whom he loves.

Q: *Give two reasons why Dido believes she must take her own life.*

A: She had broken her vows to her dead husband and had lost her self-respect because of Aeneas' rejection.

Q: *How does Dido die?*

A: She climbs onto the funeral pyre that she had tricked her sister Anna into building. Then she stabs herself with a sword that had been a gift to her from Aeneas.

EXPERT COMMENTARY

Scholar Michael Grant explains that Aeneas' visit to Carthage and his love affair with Dido, queen of Carthage, were mythical creations of story and character by Virgil:

> Virgil's most startling personal contribution to the Aeneas myth, although it has obsessed the civilised western world as a work of art, never secured acceptance in the Roman mythological canon. This was the deeply, to some almost intolerably, moving story which told how Aeneas, between his two visits to Sicily, had landed in Carthage; how the queen and founder of that city, Dido, had fallen in love with him; and how he had responded to her love, but had been compelled by the order of Jupiter to leave her and go on his destined way. And she took refuge from her sorrow in death.[6]

Further, Grant reveals the emotional dilemma Aeneas faces when he must leave Carthage and surrender to the will of the gods:

> Aeneas has to leave Dido because the voice of Jupiter and duty calls. No call of duty was ever so difficult for Aeneas to obey, or so necessary. Schoolboys have often been scandalised by reading how the hero himself declares: "I am pious Aeneas!" But that is what *pius* means, obedience to the will of the gods, the religious obedience that was to have made Rome great.
>
> The word [pious] also means loyalty to one's country—which, indeed, when one's country was Rome, seemed to be the same thing as obedience to the gods. Aeneas, like a few other mythical or legendary heroes such as Romulus and Camillus, was the *fatalis dux*, the leader who carries out the divine ordinances of Fate.
>
> In addition, the *pietas* of Aeneas refers, very specifically, to his dutifulness towards parents and kinsmen. On the whole, ethical considerations of this kind came into being rather later than religious and patriotic concepts.[7]

5

AENEAS' JOURNEY ENDS

INTRODUCTION

Aeneas left Carthage and Dido, the woman he loved, not knowing the affect her vengeful prophecy would have on the Trojans. Nor did he suspect that Juno would do all in her power to carry out the queen's dying wishes for Aeneas and his descendants and for all his beloved Trojans. Juno, still angry with Venus, was determined to defeat Aeneas and with him all the Trojans. Juno had allied herself with Queen Dido, and even though the lovely queen was now dead, Juno still did not want the Trojans to succeed in their search to find their homeland.

After leaving Carthage, the Trojan fleet stopped along the coast of Italy, near present-day Naples, and consulted with the Sibyl of Cumae. Aeneas visited the Underworld and was inspired by the ghost of his father. Sailing northward the Trojans landed in Latium, where they sailed up the Tiber River. There they met King Latinus, ruler of the region, who granted them permission to settle in the area. Soon controversy over a possible marriage between Aeneas and Lavinia, the king's daughter, lead to fighting between the newly arrived Trojans and the people of Latium. Also, Juno, determined to prevent the Trojans from claiming Latium through marriage, called on creatures from the Underworld to initiate even more fighting. The battles lasted for many years.[1]

AENEAS' JOURNEY ENDS

From far out at sea, Aeneas saw a bright glow of light coming from the shores of Carthage. But he did not know that a fire had consumed the body of his beloved Queen Dido. As he stood staring off into the distance, he heard his pilot, Palinurus, shouting to him that a storm was brewing and that they must set a course toward the coast of Sicily.

Only the year before they had encountered the same bad luck. Storms had blown the fleet from Sicily to the coast of North Africa, and now they were being blown back to Sicily again. Aeneas' only consolation was that in Sicily, he would be able to visit the grave of his father, Anchises.

The young Trojan leader was not prepared for the terrible sadness that overcame him when he visited his father's grave. To dull the ache in his heart, Aeneas organized a great festival in his father's honor. The Trojans played games, competed in athletic contests, feasted, and socialized for many months while the women tended the camp and did their daily chores. But the festivities lasted too long, and the Trojan women became restless. They began to complain to each other that they were eager to leave Sicily, find their ancestral homeland, and settle down forever.

Juno seized this opportunity to stir up trouble in the

Trojan camp. The goddess sent her messenger, Iris, disguised as an old lady, to mingle among the women. Iris convinced the women that they should stay in Sicily and make a new home. The women gathered firewood and began to burn the ships. When Aeneas saw the flames, he rushed down to the shore and offered prayers to Jupiter. Pleased that the young Trojan had finally forgotten his revelries and had come to his senses, Jupiter sent down a torrential rainstorm that extinguished the flames before all the ships could be destroyed.

At last, Aeneas realized that while the men had been

enjoying their stay in Sicily, the Trojan women were yearning to find their destined homeland. He called his men together and told them to repair the remaining ships so that they could leave the island. Venus, anxious to see the Trojans reach their true homeland, asked the sea god, Neptune, to provide calm seas for the ships until they reached the mainland of Italy. Along the Italian coast, the Trojans dropped anchor at Cumae, where Aeneas consulted with Apollo through the Sibyl of Cumae, a priestess who delivered Apollo's oracles. The Sibyl went into a trance and soon related to Aeneas that Apollo's

prophecy was very gloomy. The oracle predicted that the Trojans would experience great struggles, even war, after they landed in Italy:

The Dardan [Trojan] race will reach Lavinian country—
Put that anxiety away—but there
Will wish they had not come. Wars, vicious wars
I see ahead, and Tiber foaming blood.[2]

Aeneas assured the Sibyl that he was accustomed to hardship and that he could deal with whatever difficulties the Trojans had yet to face. He did, however, want to consult with his father, Anchises, before leaving Cumae. The Sibyl, who had access to the Underworld, took the young Trojan down into a cave and through a long tunnel. Along the way, they passed through many gates and saw horrifying visions before reaching a beautiful grassy plain where the handsome ghost of Anchises sat chatting with his ghostly friends.

Anchises was thrilled to see his son and eager for him to meet his Trojan descendants: Romulus, the founder of Rome; Numa, the second king of Rome, who would institute religious customs; Augustus Caesar, who would restore the Golden Age to Italy; and other famous Romans. He also told Aeneas that order, peace, mercy, and justice were to become Rome's gifts to mankind.

Once again, Aeneas became excited about the possibility of finding the true homeland of his people, and he asked to leave the Underworld right away. Anchises, pleased that Rome's descendants had inspired his son to complete his journey, encouraged him to leave.

So the Trojans sailed until they came to the mouth of the Tiber River, where they changed course and sailed up its calm waters. Convinced that they were home at last, women and children climbed onto the grassy riverbanks of the area called Latium and cheered. But food supplies were low, and the women were forced to make flat, tasteless pancakes to hold the freshly picked berries they placed on top. The Trojans were so hungry that they devoured the tasteless pancakes along with the fruit, just as the Harpies had predicted they would do when they reached their homeland.

Ascanius remarked:

Look, how we've devoured our tables even!

Aeneas heard his son and immediately offered a prayer to the gods.

A blessing on the land
The fates have held in store for me, a blessing
On true gods of Troy! Here is our home,
Here is our fatherland.[3]

The following day, King Latinus, ruler of Latium, greeted the Trojans and asked them why they had come. Aeneas' ambassador, Ilioneus, told the king about the fall of Troy and the Trojans' long journey to find the ancestral homeland of their people. He then offered the king many gifts, including King Priam's robes and the golden cup from which Anchises customarily drank when he made offerings to the gods. King Latinus accepted these precious gifts and gave the Trojans permission to settle.

King Latinus was pleased to meet the foreigners. In a recent vision, he had been told that his beautiful daughter, Princess Lavinia, would marry a foreigner and that the couple's descendants would make Latium a great country. The king believed Aeneas was the foreigner who was destined to marry his daughter. He was careful, however, to avoid telling Aeneas that his daughter had already been promised in marriage to Turnus, a Greek prince from a small tribe called the Rutulians that lived south of Latium. The king also withheld from Aeneas the fact that his wife, Queen Amata, was happy about the engagement.

When Juno realized that King Latinus was not only willing to allow the Trojans to settle in his land, but that he was also offering his daughter's hand in marriage to Aeneas, the goddess became angrier than she had ever been before. The Trojans had already thwarted her efforts to destroy them, and her own gods and goddesses had failed to help her. Still, Juno remained determined that the Trojans would not claim Italy through marriage, so she watched and waited for an opportunity to cause trouble. At last, Juno decided to visit the Underworld. There she sought the help of the Furies, creatures who delighted in undertaking evil chores. Juno asked the Fury named Allecto to pay a visit to Turnus, the princess' Rutulian fiancé, and warn him that Aeneas intended to marry Princess Lavinia.

Allecto did as Juno asked. She went to Turnus' palace and cautioned him that he would undoubtedly lose the princess to Aeneas if he did not drive away the Trojans. However, Turnus ignored Allecto's warning, and the old witch stormed out of the palace. Allecto then visited Ascanius, who was out hunting. She directed one of the boy's arrows at a pet deer belonging to the Rutulians. When Lavinia saw the young fawn fall to the ground, she became hysterical and ordered her attendants to find the culprit. The attendants started shooting at Ascanius and his Trojan companions. During the fighting, several Rutulian soldiers were killed.

When Turnus learned what had happened, he seized the opportunity to declare war on the Trojans. Although it was customary for a king to open the Twin Gates of War, guarded by Janus, after war was declared, King Latinus refused to acknowledge what was happening and kept the gates closed. Furious with the king and eager to get the fighting started, Juno came down and opened the gates herself.

Aeneas realized that he would need more soldiers to fight against Turnus and his men, so he sailed up the Tiber River to seek the help of King Evander, whose ancestors had been Trojans. The king welcomed Aeneas and proudly showed him his kingdom, which was little more than a village on the Tarpeian Hill. Pallas, the king's young son, offered to join Aeneas and suggested they cross the Tiber River to Etruria and seek alliance with some Etruscans who would join forces with them because they were angry with their own king.

Before Aeneas and Pallas reached the river, however, Aeneas' mother, Venus, appeared carrying a full suit of armor for her son. It had been made by Vulcan, the god of fire, at his forge. On the shield, Vulcan had hammered out scenes depicting Rome's future:

> *All these images on Vulcan's shield,*
> *His mother's gift, were wonders to Aeneas.*
> *Knowing nothing of the events themselves,*
> *He felt joy in their pictures, taking up*
> *Upon his shoulder all the destined acts*
> *And fame of his descendants.*[4]

Soon, Turnus discovered that Aeneas was away from the city of Lavinium, and he organized his men, who attacked with force. But the Trojans remained inside the walls of the city and did not respond. Turnus attacked a second time. Still, the Trojans refused to respond. Turnus, unaware that Aeneas had instructed his men to refrain from fighting until he returned with additional forces, set the Trojans' ships on fire in an effort to draw the Trojan men out of the city. But Jupiter, who had been watching over Aeneas' men, turned the ships into sea nymphs and sent them bobbing out to sea.

The following day, when Turnus attacked Lavinium for the third time, the Trojans threw open the gates of the city and came storming out, hurling rocks and spears at the Rutulian soldiers. Turnus rode boldly into the city ahead of his men and cut down every Trojan soldier in sight. The tall Rutulian warrior frightened the remaining Trojans, and they retreated, until one of the soldiers reminded the others that they were running away from only one man. Turnus' presence had been so majestic that the Trojan men had not realized that he was riding alone. Suddenly, they turned around and charged at him. Turnus backed away toward the Tiber and jumped into the river, wearing all his armor.

Aeneas, who had by now succeeded in organizing a large contingent of Etruscan soldiers in addition to Evander's men from the area of the Tarpeian Hill, returned home and joined the fighting. He saw Turnus, who had come out of the water and was chasing Evander's son, Pallas. But before Aeneas could help the boy, Turnus had driven his spear through the young man's chest, taken Pallas' ornate sword belt, and slung it over his own shoulder. Evander threw himself on his son's body and wept.

Suddenly, Aeneas' sadness turned to rage. He plunged into the battle and killed as many Rutulian soldiers as he could find. The killing went on for many days until, at last, both sides agreed to a truce so that they could bury the dead.

Evander, still mourning the death of Pallas, did not regret that he had given the Trojans land in Latium—but he wanted Aeneas to avenge his son's death by fighting Turnus one-on-one and killing him.

Unfortunately, the war went on for many years until, at last, Turnus' Latin allies held a meeting and agreed to withdraw their support from the Rutulians because Turnus' battle was becoming impossible to win. Their decision angered Turnus, who organized his remaining forces and returned to battle once again.

Juno, who had been watching the battles from high above the golden clouds, realized that Turnus was doomed. At last, she appealed to her husband, Jupiter, to allow the Latins to retain their name and language and, in exchange, she would put an end to the war:

> *I yield now and for all my hatred leave*
> *This battlefield. But one thing not retained*
> *By fate I beg for Latium, for the future*
> *Greatness of your kin: when presently*
> *They crown peace with a happy wedding day—*
> *So let it be—and merge their laws and treaties,*
> *. . . Let Latium be.*
> *Let there be Alban kings for generations,*
> *And let Italian valor be the strength*
> *Of Rome in after times. Once and for all*
> *Troy fell, and with her name let her lie fallen.*[5]

Jupiter agreed to grant Juno her wish. He assured her that the marriage between Latins and Trojans would produce an indomitable race. Through the marriage of Livinia and Aeneas—it was implied—their descendants would embody the strength, courage, and virtue of the people from whom they came.

Meanwhile, Turnus continued to be defeated on the battlefield. Eventually, however, the arrogant young Rutulian agreed to deal with Aeneas. Aeneas, pleased to be able to fulfill his promise to King Evander to avenge the death of Pallas, made the necessary arrangements. On the day of the face-off, Turnus mistakenly picked up the wrong sword, and when he swung at Aeneas, it shattered against the heavy shield made for Aeneas by Vulcan.

Turnus called to his men to bring him his proper sword, but it was too late. Aeneas pinned the jealous warrior to the ground and ran his spear through one of his thighs. Turnus knew that the next stab would be into his chest, and before he died, he begged Aeneas to return his body to his father for proper burial. Aeneas hesitated for a moment, and even considered sparing Turnus' life, but then his eyes fixed on young Pallas' sword belt slung over Turnus' shoulder and his heart turned cold. Without hesitation, Aeneas thrust his sword into Turnus' chest and killed him.

After Turnus' death, the fighting ended and Latins and Trojans began to live together in peace. The subsequent marriage of Aeneas and Princess Lavinia gave the Roman people the Trojan ancestry they so desired.

QUESTIONS AND ANSWERS

Q: *After Aeneas descended into the Underworld, his father told him that Rome would give several important gifts to the world. What were they?*

A: Order, peace, mercy, and justice.

Q: *Why did King Latinus want his daughter to marry Aeneas?*

A: In a dream, the king learned that his daughter was destined to marry a foreigner, and that their descendants would make Latium a great country.

Q: *To whom was Princess Lavinia betrothed before the Trojans arrived?*

A: Turnus, a young Rutulian from a nearby tribe.

Q: *What happened to the Trojan fleet after Turnus' men set it on fire?*

A: Jupiter turned the ships into sea nymphs and sent them bobbing out to sea.

Q: *Why was Juno unable to prevent the founding of Rome? Why did she persist in harassing the Trojans?*

A: The ultimate victory of the Trojans in Italy was decreed by fate and could not be changed. Juno instigated war on behalf of Dido, who wanted revenge on the Trojans.

Q: *What overall effect did the gods and goddesses have on Aeneas' journey and what did they symbolize in the tale?*

A: They took part in the story's action to illustrate that there was a divine plan that controlled Roman history.

They also served to symbolize human character: Venus was a kind protector; Juno was angry and vengeful; and Jupiter was always in control because he had power over all the gods.

Q: *Is Aeneas a believable character? Explain.*

A: Because Aeneas represented everything that Romans considered noble in human nature, he appears very real and people easily identify with him.

EXPERT COMMENTARY

In his book *Aeneas, Sicily, and Rome*, Professor G. Karl
Galinsky sheds light on the background of *The Aeneid* by
suggesting that Virgil helped form the image of the pious
Aeneas:

> [I]t suffices to say that by the end of the first century B.C.
> Trojan descent had been the jealously guarded prerogative
> [right, or privilege] of a few noble families, *familiae
> Troianae*, for the better part of two centuries. Therefore
> there was at least the possibility that another hero might
> have been accepted as the popular ancestor of all the
> Roman people. But since it was Octavian, a member of the
> Julian family, who asked Virgil to write the epic, Aeneas
> was selected because of his assumed connection with the
> gens [family, or clan] Julia, and once the choice was made,
> all the power of Augustan propaganda was used to publi-
> cize it and make the Aeneas legend popular.[6]

Michael Grant, in his book *Roman Myths*, says that
Virgil's story of the Aeneas saga reassures the Romans that
a thousand years of myth and history are reaching their
climax in the imperial mission of Augustan Rome.

> Everything that Virgil says, every one of his unequaled
> dramatic resources, is mobilised to stress and illustrate the
> continuity between that mythical time and his own day, to
> make recent events the culmination of the mythic-historical
> process, and to display the indissoluble connection
> between the men he was writing for and the heroes he was
> writing about.[7]

6

ROMULUS AND REMUS

INTRODUCTION

According to some legends, Rome was founded by Romulus, one of the twin sons of Mars. The first mention of the Romulus and Remus myth was made by a Sicilian historian named Alcimus in the fourth century B.C.[1] Thereafter, variants of the myth began to appear. The Romulus and Remus myth won favor among the Roman people because it gave them an immortal ancestor—Mars.

The legend of Romulus and Remus began with King Proca, the thirteenth king of Rome. Proca had two sons, Numitor and Amulius, who vied for the throne. Numitor was the older son and the rightful successor to the throne, but the younger brother, Amulius, seized the throne and sent Numitor to live on a small farm nearby. Amulius then had Numitor's sons killed and his daughter, Rhea Silvia, banished to the temple of Vesta. As a Vestal Virgin, Rhea Silvia vowed to remain chaste for thirty years, thus assuring that she would have no heirs. In a curious turn of events, however, Rhea Silvia gave birth to twins. Eventually, the twins would find their grandfather, Numitor; help to defeat their uncle, Amulius; and become the future successors to the throne.[2]

ROMULUS AND REMUS

King Amulius was furious. His had just learned that his niece, Rhea Silvia, had given birth to twins even though she was a Vestal Virgin and had vowed to remain chaste. The king paced up and down the palace corridors trying to decide what he should do. Finally reaching a decision, he ordered his men to bring Rhea Silvia to him.

When his men returned, the king was sitting in the throne room on his ornately carved chair, his face flushed with rage. The men shoved the frail young woman toward the king, and she slumped in a heap on the floor. King Amulius looked at his young niece and snapped, "Mars, you say? The god of war made you with child? Am I to believe such an impossible story?"

As Rhea Silvia looked up at her uncle, her sad, green eyes filled with tears. She pleaded, "You must believe me. Mars is the father of my twins. He took me against my will in the gods' sacred grove. It is not my fault."

With no pity and little remorse, Amulius got up from his great chair and walked toward the door. As he left the regal throne room, he muttered, "There will never be an heir to this throne. Never." Then, turning to his men, he ordered, "Take her away, and see that she and the twins are thrown into the Tiber River. And be quick."

Rhea Silvia was terrified as the king's men snatched

the basket in which her sons slept peacefully and dragged her and the innocent infants down to the river. Weeks of rain had caused the river to overflow its banks, and it was obvious that there were many deep sections in which Rhea Silvia and her babies could easily drown in the fast-flowing water.

The king's men carried out their grisly deed, disposing of the mother and children in the river. The young woman was unable to stay afloat, and soon her limp body was washed down the river and out to sea. Somehow, though, the basket carrying her twin boys drifted down the river until it became caught in the roots of an olive tree jutting out from the banks. When their basket stopped its gentle swaying movements from being carried along the current, the twins began to cry.

A she-wolf hunting along the river's edge followed the sound of their cries until she discovered the twins in their basket. The she-wolf rubbed her soft snout against their bodies until they stopped crying. Then, she carefully lifted them, one at a time, from their woven basket and carried them back to her cave on the hillside overlooking the river. Throughout many nights, she warmed and comforted the little babies, allowing them to nurse from her whenever they grew hungry.

One day, Faustulus, a shepherd for King Amulius, was walking along the banks of the Tiber when he spotted a she-wolf out hunting. Believing this she-wolf had been responsible for stealing several of his lost sheep, he followed her back to her hillside cave. But instead of lost sheep, Faustulus saw two young boys in the shelter of the cave. At once, Faustulus realized they were the answer to his prayers. The young shepherd and his wife had been childless for many years; here were the children they had

dreamed about. "I will wait," he whispered to himself. "I will wait until the boys are left alone."

As dusk approached, the she-wolf left her cave to do the day's hunting. As soon as she had gone, Faustulus sneaked inside the cave and gathered up the babies. He tucked one little boy under each arm and raced home to his wife, Laurentia. When she saw the two beautiful baby boys, Laurentia was overcome with joy. Quickly, she made a small bed in one corner of their tiny hut, lined it with thick sheepskins, and began tending to the children's every need. The couple named them Romulus and Remus. Days turned into months and months into years. The twin boys were diligent sons who helped to care for the house and tended the sheep with their father.

As they grew older, however, the boys grew bored with shepherding. One day, Remus suggested to his brother that they follow a band of local robbers who stole from farms in the area. Remus' plan was to steal from the robbers and distribute the loot among their friends.

Romulus, on the other hand, believed that his brother's game was dangerous and was reluctant to go along with the plan. Eventually, however, he was persuaded to join his brother. Romulus followed Remus to the robbers' lair. The boys carried away fresh fruits and vegetables, tools, and whatever valuables they could find, and herded up some stolen sheep, as well. Together they took the booty off to distribute among their friends. The game was fun—they liked robbing the robbers. But one day when Remus was out alone, one of the robbers came back to his lair, grabbed him, and twisted his arm behind his back. "You will pay for this," the robber sneered at Remus, "and you will be punished by the king himself."

Remus began to sweat as the robber dragged him down the road to the king's palace. The angry robber pounded hard on the palace door until an attendant finally opened it. "The king must see this thief. Take me to him," the robber demanded in such a loud and confident voice that the attendant was too startled to argue. Puzzled, the attendant led the man to the elegant chamber of the king.

In his most humble and respectful voice, the robber said, "Sire, I have caught a thief who dares to steal sheep from your brother Numitor's herd," lied the robber, who had made up the story hoping that the king would put the boy to death.

The king thought the situation over for a moment and said with impatience, "I have no time for young thieves. Take him to my brother. He can do the punishing."

The attendant quickly pushed Remus and the robber out the palace door and pointed in the direction of Numitor's house. As the men approached the house, the robber called out, "Brother of the king, come out. King Amulius has asked me to deliver the boy who has been stealing your sheep."

When Numitor opened the door of his house, he was shocked. There, dressed in shabby clothes, stood a handsome young boy with an unmistakable likeness to his dead daughter, Rhea Silvia. But before the king's brother could speak, the robber began, "This is the boy who stole your sheep. I caught him, and King Amulius has given you the task of punishing him." Then, the robber added slyly, "Perhaps you will reward me for my efforts, Sire?"

But before Numitor could respond, the shepherd Faustulus, accompanied by a second young man almost identical to the first, came tramping into the house. Numitor staggered backward. Rhea Silvia's piercing green eyes shone from this young man's face, too. The old man realized that he was face-to-face with the two grown grandsons he had thought were dead. Tears came to

Numitor's eyes as he muttered, "You are my grandsons, the twin sons of my dear daughter Rhea Silvia and the god Mars. Oh, dear children, where have you been?"

For the first time, the poor shepherd Faustulus realized that the babies he had taken from the she-wolf on the banks of the Tiber were no ordinary children but the sons of a royal princess and a god. Shaking with fear, Faustulus explained what had happened and asked Numitor's forgiveness for having kept the boys and raised them as his own.

Then Numitor explained that he, not King Amulius, was the rightful king of Alba Longa and that his brother had stolen the throne. All at once, the humble shepherd replied, "But Amulius has not succeeded. Happily, your heirs have survived, and with our help, you will regain the throne."

Later that evening, Faustulus, the twins, and a group of neighboring shepherds gathered in Numitor's courtyard. They waited until darkness enveloped the palace. Then, they crept into the chamber of King Amulius and took him by surprise. The king called out for his men, but before they could arrive, the shepherds, led by Numitor and the twins, killed King Amulius.

Numitor, his twin grandsons, Faustulus, and Laurentia went to live in the palace. Numitor was so grateful to the couple for having taken such good care of his grandsons that he treated them as part of the royal family. Romulus and Remus were happy because they had been reunited with their grandfather, and they did not have to leave their doting adoptive parents.

Numitor appeared before his people and explained that he was their rightful ruler. He told how his evil brother had usurped the throne many years before. He also disclosed his brother's plot to eliminate all heirs to the throne and explained that Amulius had been killed by men who were defending themselves, not for revenge.

Numitor quickly resumed his place on the throne, and the people rejoiced. After many years, Alba Longa prospered and expanded under Numitor's exemplary rule, so much so that King Numitor asked his twin grandsons to build another city nearby to ease the overcrowding. However, as their grandfather and uncle had done, the twins argued about who would be ruler. Since they were twins and neither could claim to be the elder, the boys agreed to hold a competition to resolve the issue. They agreed to let the gods decide the winner and send down an omen indicating their choice for the ruler of the new city.

"I will wait for a sign from the gods on Palatine Hill," said Romulus.

"And I will wait on Aventine Hill," said Remus.

Shortly thereafter, six large, black vultures landed on Aventine Hill, and Remus was very happy. Then, twelve large, black vultures landed on Palatine Hill, and Romulus cheered. Remus' followers argued that because the first vultures had landed on their hill, Remus should be the ruler. In contrast, Romulus' followers argued that because the greater number of vultures had landed on Palatine Hill, Romulus should be the ruler.

Some legends tell of a terrible battle between the two brothers and their people and that Remus was killed during the fighting. The most popular legend tells that Romulus was certain that he should be the new king, so he had an earthen wall built around Palatine Hill. To show Romulus that a wall was no threat to him, Remus jumped over it. Remus' defiance angered his brother so much that he flew into a rage and killed him. Romulus then warned

Remus' followers that the same fate would befall anyone else who dared to jump over the wall.

Soon afterward, Romulus was proclaimed king and a new city was built on Palatine Hill. The city was named Rome, after its celebrated founder.

QUESTIONS AND ANSWERS

Q: *Who were Numitor and Amulius?*

A: They were the sons of King Proca, the twelfth king of Alba Longa.

Q: *How did Amulius become king, and what did he do to Numitor and his children?*

A: Amulius seized Numitor's throne but did not kill him. Amulius had Numitor's two sons killed and sent Rhea Silvia to the temple of Vesta to be sure she would have no heirs.

Q: *If Rhea Silvia was a Vestal Virgin, how did she manage to bear twin sons?*

A: Rhea Silvia claimed to have been taken against her will by Mars, the god of war.

Q: *What was King Amulius' reaction when he heard that Rhea Silvia had twin sons?*

A: King Amulius was furious when he discovered his niece had given birth to twins. He ordered that Rhea Silvia and her babies be drowned in the Tiber River to assure that they would never be a threat to his throne.

Q: *Who saved the twins?*

A: A she-wolf heard their cries, took them back to her cave, and nursed them until they were able to eat solid food.

Q: *Who adopted the twins after the she-wolf?*

A: A shepherd named Faustulus and his wife, Laurentia, brought up the twins as if they were the couple's own children.

Q: *How did Numitor discover that his grandsons were still alive?*

A: Romulus arrived at Numitor's house at the very same time that Remus was being accused by a scheming robber of having stolen Numitor's sheep. Numitor recognized the unmistakable likeness of Rhea Silvia in the faces of Romulus and Remus. He knew that they were his grandsons.

Q: *How did the twins' relationship repeat history?*

A: The twins argued and fought over the right to rule just as their grandfather, Numitor, and his brother, Amulius, had done.

Q: *What was the sign sent by the gods to determine the new location of the capital?*

A: The arrival of vultures that landed on the site of the chosen city.

Q: *Why is the capital of Italy named Rome?*

A: According to this legend, Palatine Hill, where Romulus lived, became the gods' choice for the beginning of the new capital city. The city was named Rome in honor of Romulus.

EXPERT COMMENTARY

Myths about the founding of Rome by Aeneas, and those told about Romulus and Remus, vied for popularity among the Romans:

> During the fourth and early third centuries B.C. Romulus gained the upper hand over Aeneas as the supposed city-founder. Then, in the Punic Wars, new factors revived the Aeneas saga. But interest in Romulus and Remus still continued to grow, and successive versions progressively became more elaborate.[3]
>
> The rape of Rhea Silvia or Ilia by Mars, which was said to have taken place in the god's sacred grove, is a story that has parallels in many cultures, going back at least as far as the Bronze Age. It is a prestige myth, to invest the birth and deeds of a popular hero with an aura of mystery and wonder; the sort of tale which exploits the ambiguous borderline between gods and human beings.[4]

Ancient stories about abandoned children were popular among the mythologies of many cultures and the story of Romulus and Remus was used as a symbol of Rome's growing power:

> Babies being abandoned in the wild, then being saved by an animal or country worker and then returning to take their rightful place in society is a common one in myth. In Greek myth, Oedipus was exposed on the mountainside. In fairytales it is common for babies, or older children like Snow White and Hansel and Gretel, to be abandoned in the woods.[5]

ROMAN MYTHOLOGY ▣ TIMELINE ▣

From 1000 B.C.—Settlements in Italy

1250 B.C.—The Trojan War

1176 B.C.—Aeneas founds Lavinium in Latium

1152 B.C.—Ascanius, son of Aeneas, rules Alba Longa preceding Rome's founding; King Proca of Alba Longa fathers Numitor and Amulius

753 B.C.—Founding of Rome by Romulus

715–673 B.C.—Reign of Numa Pompilius

673–642 B.C.—Reign of Tullus Hostilius

642–617 B.C.—Reign of Ancus Marcius

616–578 B.C.—Reign of Tarquinius Priscus (Tarquin the First)

578–534 B.C.—Reign of Servius Tullius

534–510 B.C.—Reign of Tarquinius Superbus (Tarquin the Proud); Fall of the monarchy

510–476 B.C.—Period of the Republic

387 B.C.–Gauls sack and burn Rome and most of Rome's official documents are consumed by fire

264–146 B.C.—Punic Wars

218 B.C.—Rome conquers Etruria

49–44 B.C.—Julius Caesar dictator of Rome

27 B.C.–A.D. 14—Augustus first emperor of Rome[1]

ROMAN AND GREEK GODS AND GODDESSES

Roman Name	Description	Greek Name
Aeolus	God of the winds	Aeolus
Apollo	God of light, music, prophecy, intellect, arts, and healing	Apollo
Ceres	Goddess of agriculture, and fertility	Demeter
Cupid	God of love; son of Venus	Eros
Diana	Goddess of the wildwood, lady of beasts, goddess of the moon, marriage, and childbirth	Artemis
Janus	God of doorways, journeys, and beginnings	No equivalent
Juno	Queen of the goddesses; consort of Jupiter; goddess of women and motherhood	Hera
Jupiter/Jove	King of the gods; god of the sky; father of gods and men	Zeus
Mars	God of war	Ares
Mercury	Divine messenger; God of trade and communications	Hermes
Minerva	Goddess of wisdom, crafts, and power	Athena
Neptune	God of the sea	Poseidon
Saturn	God of agriculture; Ruler of the Golden Age	Cronus
Vesta	Goddess of the hearth, and fire	Hestia
Vulcan	God of fire and the forge	Hephaestus
Venus	Goddess of love and beauty	Aphrodite

CERES

MERCURY

MINERVA

JANUS

NEPTUNE

MARS

VENUS

JUNO

JUPITER

APOLLO

DIANA

🔳 GLOSSARY 🔳

Achates (ah-*kay*-teez)—The companion of Aeneas.

Aeneas (ah-*nee*-us)—Son of the goddess Venus and the mortal Anchises; fled Troy and settled the Trojan people in Italy where he wed a Latin princess; Roman national hero.

Aeolus (ee-*oh*-lus)—King of the winds.

Alba Longa (*al*-buh *lon*-guh)—A town in Latium; birthplace of Romulus and Remus.

Allecto (al-*lehk*-toh)—A Fury who, at Juno's request, incites war between the Trojans and the Latins.

Amulius (am-*you*-lee-us)—Son of King Proca; king of Alba Longa; brother of Numitor.

Anchises (an-*ky*-seez)—The father of Aeneas.

Apollo (ah-*pahl*-loh)—The god of prophecy, light, truth, and civilization; favors the Trojans' mission to find their ancestral homeland.

Ascanius (as-*kay*-nee-us)—The son of Aeneas and Creüsa.

Aventine (*ah*-vin-teen)—One of the hills of Rome.

Consuls (*kon*-suls)—One of two chief magistrates of the ancient Roman Republic.

Crete (kreet)—A large island in the Mediterranean Sea located southeast of Greece.

Creüsa (kray-*ooh*-suh)—First wife of Aeneas; mother of Ascanius.

Cupid (*kyoo*-pihd)—The god of love; son of Venus.

Dido (*dy*-doh)—The queen of Carthage; fell in love with Aeneas on his way to Italy.

Evander (ee-*van*-duhr)—Pallas' father, who allies himself with Aeneas.

Furies (*fyoor*-ees)—Avenging spirits who drive their victims mad with rage or instill terror in those about to die.

Harpies (*har*-pees)—Monsters that are part bird and part woman.

Janus (*jay*-nus)—The god of beginnings, represented as having two faces—one facing forward and the other facing backward.

Juno (*jyoo*-noh)—The queen of the gods and Jupiter's wife; the Trojans' most powerful opponent.

Jupiter (*jyoo*-pih-tur)—The king of the gods and Juno's husband; he regulates the actions of all gods and favors the Trojans.

Lares (*lar*-eez)—Agricultural spirits that brought prosperity and well-being to the families of early farmers and sheep herders; they later became household spirits.

Latinus (*lah*-tee-nus)—The king of Latium; Aeneas' father-in-law.

Latium (lah-*tee*-um)—The region of central Italy that includes Rome.

Lavinia (lah-*vihn*-ee-uh)—Second wife of Aeneas; daughter of King Latinus.

Lavinium (luh-*vihn*-ee-um)—The first Trojan settlement in Italy, twenty miles south of present-day Rome; it was founded by Aeneas.

Livy (*lee*-vee)—A historian (59 B.C.–A.D. 17) who wrote a history of Rome in 142 volumes, including events from Aeneas' departure from Troy to the birth of Romulus and Remus, and the reigns of Rome's seven kings.

Mars (marz)—The god of war; father of Romulus and Remus.

Mercury (*muhr*-kyoo-ree)—The messenger of the gods.

Neptune (*nep*-toon)—The god of the sea.

Numitor (*noo*-ma-tor)—A son of King Proca; king of Alba Longa; grandfather of Romulus and Remus.

Nymphs (nimpfs)—Female nature spirits.

Octavian (oc-*tay*-vee-in)—The adopted son (63 B.C.–A.D. 14) of Julius Caesar, who became the first Roman emperor in 27 B.C. and was given the title "Augustus."

Ovid (*ahv*-id)—Publius Ovidius Naso (43 B.C.–A.D. 17), Roman poet and author of many books, including *Metamorphoses* and *Fasti*.

Palatine (*pal*-ah-teen)—One of the hills of Rome.

Pales (*pa*-lez)—A rustic divinity; protector of the flock; he was honored at Parilia.

Pallas (*pal*-luhs)—Evander's son, whose death by Turnus' hand was avenged by Aeneas.

Parilia (par-*il*-ee-ah)—Festival of Pales, held on April 21.

Penates (pe-*nay*-teez)—Household spirits that were

responsible for keeping the cupboard well stocked and the family healthy.

Priam (*pree*-am)—The king of Troy.

Remus (*ree*-mus)—The twin brother of Romulus; son of Mars and Rhea Silvia.

Rhea Silvia (*ree*-ah *sil*-vee-ah)—The daughter of Numitor; mother of twin sons Romulus and Remus.

Romulus (*rom*-you-lus)—The founder of Rome; twin brother of Remus; son of Mars and Rhea Silvia.

Rutulian (roo-*tul*-ee-an)—An ancient people of Latium, with capital at Ardea; in legend, the people of Turnus.

Sibyl (*sib*-ul)—A soothsayer or someone who foretells future events by some sort of supernatural means.

Tiber (*ty*-bur) River—The largest river in Italy; it flows out of the Apennine Mountains, past the city of Rome, and into the Tyrennian Sea.

Trojans (*tro*-juns)—The people of Troy.

Troy—A city in northwest Asia Minor; scene of legendary ten-year siege by Greek armies.

Turnus (*toor*-nus)—A Rutulian prince and leader of the forces who opposed the Trojan settlement in Latium; Aeneas' strongest Latin opponent.

Tyre (teer)—An ancient Phoenician seaport on the present-day coast of Lebanon.

Underworld—The realm of the dead.

Venus (*vee*-nus)—The goddess of love and the mother of Aeneas by her mortal lover Anchises.

Vesta (*ves*-tah)—The goddess of the hearth, perhaps originally as a deity of the individual domestic hearth, then as the deity of the king's hearth on behalf of the whole people.

Vestal Virgins (*ves*-tal *vir*-jinz)—The virgin priestesses of Vesta who tended the sacred flame.

Virgil (*vur*-jul)—The Roman poet Publius Vergilius Maro (70–19 B.C.) composed the Aeneid, an epic poem about the founding of Rome by a young Trojan named Aeneas.

Vulcan (*vuhl*-kun)—The god of fire and metalworking; husband of Venus; made a set of armor for Aeneas.

▤ Chapter Notes ▤

Preface

1. Michael Grant, *Roman Myths* (New York: Charles Scribner's Sons, 1971), p.221.

2. Ibid., pp.221–222.

3. Roy Willis, ed., *Mythology: An Illustrated Encyclopedia* (New York: Barnes and Noble, 1993), p. 170.

4. Grant, pp. 6–13.

5. Georges Dumezil, *Archaic Roman Religion*, vol. 1 (Baltimore: The John Hopkins University Press, 1996), p. 370.

6. Ibid., pp. 330–333.

7. Ibid., pp. 341–346.

8. Ibid., pp. 342–355.

9. Mark P. O. Morford and Robert J. Lenardon, *Classical Mythology*, 6th edition (New York: Longman, Inc., 1999), p. 513.

10. Ibid., p. 519.

11. "Early History of Rome; Roman heroes and hero-ines," n.d., <http://www/luc.edu/faculty/ldossey/3081ect1.htm> (January 27, 2001).

12. "The History or Etruria," n.d., <http://pages.ancientsites.com/~Camitlnas_Tullius/history2.html> (October 6, 2000).

13. "The Sibylline Books," n.d., <http://www.csus.edu/indiv/v/vonmeirk/8-045SI.html> (January 30, 2001).

14. "Latium and the Beginnings of Rome in the Seventh Century B. C.," n.d., <http://myron.sjsu.edu/romeweb/GLOSSARY/timeln/t12.htm> (November 9, 2000).

15. Roy Willis, ed., *Mythology: An Illustrated Guide* (New York: Barnes and Noble, 1998), p. 171.

16. Ibid., p. 167.

17. Richard Cavendish, ed., *Mythology: An Illustrated Encyclopedia* (New York: Barnes and Noble, 1993), p. 143.

18. Anthony Marks and Graham Tingay, *The Romans* (London: Usborne Publishing, Ltd., 1990), p. 91.

19. "Livy," n.d., <http://homer.reed.edu/Livy.html> (November 9, 2000)

20. "Aeneas, the Alban Kings, and the Twins: A Problem of Chronology," (December 17, 1995), <http://ccat.sas.upenn.edu/~awiesner/vergil/comm2/legend/chronology.html> (November 9, 2000).

Chapter 1. The Capitoline Triad: Jupiter, Juno, and Minerva

1. Mark P. O. Morford and Robert J. Lenardon, *Classical Mythology,* 6th edition (New York: Longman, Inc., 1999), p. 509.

2. "The History of Etruria," n.d., <http://pages.ancientsites.com/~Camitlnas_Tullius/history2.html> (October 6, 2000).

3. Stewart Perowne, *Roman Mythology* (New York: The Hamlyn Publishing Group, Limited, 1969), pp. 17–18.

4. Simon Hornblower and Antony Spawford, eds., *Oxford Classical Encyclopedia* (New York: Oxford University Press, 1996), pp. 801–802.

5. Morford and Lenardon, pp. 506–508.

6. "Gods and Goddesses of Rome," n.d., <http://www.novaroma.org/rekugui_romana/deities.html> (October 2, 2000).

7. Morford and Lenardon, p. 509.

8. Ibid.

9. Perowne, pp. 16–17.

10. Morford and Lenardon, pp. 507–508.

11. Jane F. Gardner, *Roman Myths* (Austin: University of Texas Press, 1993), pp.13–14.

Chapter 2. Roman Deities: Mars, Venus, and Apollo

1. Georges Dumezil, *Archaic Roman Religion*, vol. 1 (Baltimore: The Johns Hopkins University Press, 1996), pp. 205–245.

2. Mark P. O. Morford and Robert J. Lenardon, *Classical Mythology*, 6th edition (New York: Longman, Inc., 1999), pp. 514–515.

3. "Paris," *Encyclopedia Mythica*, n.d., <http://www .pantheon.org/mythica/articles/p/paris.html> (November 9, 2000).

4. Cora E. Miley, *Myths and Legends of Greece and Rome* (New York: Harlow Publishing Co., 1926), p. 56.

5. Steward Perowne, *Roman Mythology* (New York: Hamlyn Publishing Group Limited, 1969), p. 21.

6. "Calendar of Roman Religion," n.d., <http:// members.aol.com/hlabadjr/RELIGIO2b.HTM> (October 2, 2000).

7. Morford and Lenardon, p. 522.

Chapter 3. Aeneas' Journey to Crete

1. Virgil, *Aeneid*, trans. Robert Fitzgerald (New York: Vantage Books, 1984), pp. 65–91.

2. Ibid., p. 68.

3. Ibid., p. 71.

4. G. Karl Galinsky, *Aeneas, Sicily, and Rome* (Princeton, New Jersey: Princeton University Press, 1969), pp. 52–53.

5. Ibid., p. 61.

6. Virgil, *Aeneid*, trans. John Henry Humphries (New York: Charles Scribner's Sons, 1984), p. viii.

Chapter 4. Aeneas Meets Dido

1. Virgil, *Aeneid*, trans. Robert Fitzgerald (New York: Random House, 1984), p. 12.

2. Ibid., p. 106.

3. Ibid., p. 109.

4. Ibid., pp. 118–119.

5. Ibid., p. 120.

6. Ibid.

7. Michael Grant, *Roman Myths* (New York: Charles Scribner's Sons, 1971), p. 83.

8. Ibid., pp. 86–87.

Chapter 5. Aeneas' Journey Ends

1. Virgil, *Aeneid*, trans. Robert Fitzgerald (New York: Random House, 1984), pp. 93–402.

2. Ibid., p. 162.

3. Ibid., p. 199.

4. Ibid., p. 256.

5. Ibid., pp. 397–398.

6. G. Karl Galinsky, *Aeneas, Sicily, and Rome* (Princeton, New Jersey: Princeton University Press, 1969), pp. 52–53.

7. Michael Grant, *Roman Myths* (New York: Charles Scribner's Sons, 1971), p. 67.

Chapter 6. Romulus and Remus

1. Michael Grant, *Roman Myths* (New York: Charles Scribner's Sons, 1971), p. 99.

2. Grant, pp. 91–116.

3. Ibid., p. 99.

4. Ibid., p. 100.

5. Cotterell, Arthur, ed. *World Mythology* (Bristol, England: Dempsey Parr, 1999), p. 71.

▤ FURTHER READING ▤

Bulfinch, Thomas. *Bulfinch's Mythology*. New York: The Modern Library, 1998.

Cavendish, Richard, ed. *Mythology: An Illustrated Encyclopedia*. New York: Barnes and Noble, 1993.

Cotterell, Arthur, ed. *Encyclopedia of Mythology*. New York: Lorenz Books, 2000.

Dupont, Florence. *Daily Life in Ancient Rome*. Cambridge, Mass.: Blackwell Publishers, 1989.

Gardner, Jane F. *Roman Myths*. Austin: University of Texas Press, 1993.

Grant, Michael. *Roman Myths*. New York: Charles Scribner's Sons, 1971.

Guerber, H. A. *The Myths of Greece and Rome*. New York: Dover Publications, 1993.

Hornblower, Simon and Anthony Spawforth. *Oxford Classical Dictionary*. New York: Oxford University Press, 1996.

Marks, Anthony and Graham Tingay. *The Romans*. London: Usborne Publishing Ltd., 1990.

Morford, Mark P. O. and Robert J. Lenardon. *Classical Mythology*. Reading, Mass. Addison-Wesley Longman, Inc., 1999.

Perowne, Stewart. *Roman Mythology*. New York: The Hamlyn Publishing Group Ltd., 1969.

Pickles, Dwayne E. *Roman Myths, Heroes, and Legends.* Philadelphia, Pa.: Chelsea House Publishers, 1999.

Scarres, Christopher. *The Penguin Historical Atlas of Ancient Rome.* New York: Viking Penguin, 1995.

Scullard, H. H. *Festivals and Ceremonies of the Roman Republic.* Ithaca, New York: Cornell University Press, 1981.

Virgil. *Aeneid.* trans., Robert Fitzgerald. New York: Vintage Books, 1984.

Willis, Roy, ed. *Mythology: An Illustrated Guide.* New York: Barnes and Noble, 1998.

INTERNET ADDRESSES

Bulfinch's Mythology

<http://www.bulfinch.org/fables/welcome.html>

MythMan's Roman Mythology Today

<http://romanmyth.com>

⊟ INDEX ⊟

12   11/05